THE BEST FLEA, ANTIQUE, VINTAGE, AND NEW-STYLE MARKETS IN AMERICA

THE BEST FLEA, ANTIQUE, VINTAGE, AND NEW-STYLE MARKETS IN AMERICA
Pamela Keech

The Little Bookroom ⚲ New York

Photos © Pamela Keech (unless noted below)
Cover Photograph: Annie Schlechter
Cover Design: Evan Johnston
Design: Nancy Ng
Additional photo credits: Rose Bowl-Jaime Burton-Oare, Jaime Burton-Oare (The Rose Bowl Flea Market); Paige K. Parsons (Alameda Point Antiques Faire); *The Walnut Bureau* (Walnut Antique Show); Pam Knecht (Plucky Maidens Junk Fest); Kate Jennings (The Farm Chicks Antique Show)

While every effort has been made by the author and the publisher to ensure that the information contained in this guide is accurate, they accept no responsibility for any inconvenience, loss, damage, costs, or expenses of any nature whatsoever incurred or suffered by anyone as a result of any advice or information contained in this guide.

Library of Congress Cataloging-in-Publication Data

Keech, Pamela.
The best flea, antique, vintage, and new-style markets in America / by Pamela Keech.

pages cm
Includes index.
ISBN 978-1-936941-04-9 (alk. paper)
1. Flea markets--United States. 2. Antiques--United States. 3. Antique dealers--United States. I. Title.
HF5482.15.K44 2013
381'.1920973--dc23
2013009846

Printed in the United States of America

Published by The Little Bookroom
435 Hudson Street, Suite 300
New York NY 10014
editorial@littlebookroom.com
www.littlebookroom.com

ISBN 978-1-936941-04-9

2 4 6 8 0 9 7 5 3 1

For Nicholas Prince,
who said the two things one must always have in the house are champagne and fireworks.

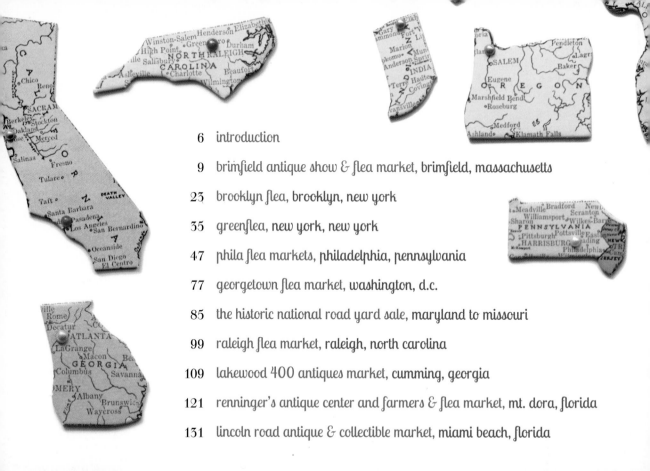

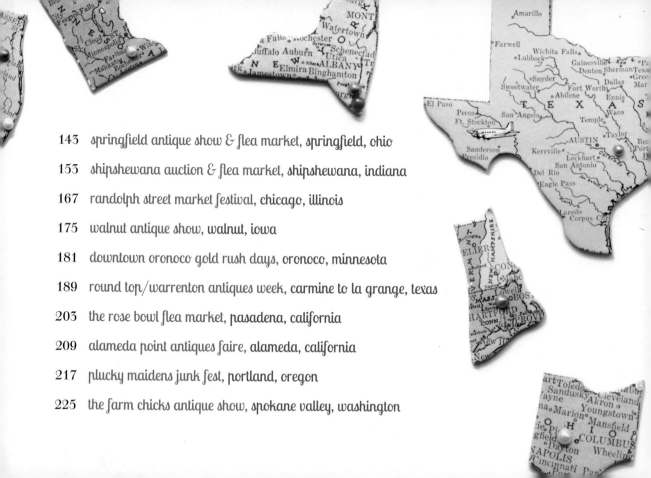

introduction

What's up with flea and antique markets? You hear their salad days are over, then the Brooklyn Flea pops up and smacks you right on the nose. Repercussions are banging across the country. Vintage is bigger than ever and established markets like Springfield, Ohio are adding special sections for vintage and remade goods. The Plucky Maidens in Oregon are so hooked on junk they take side trips to London and Paris to find more. Can we go too?

Don't believe the rumors that all the good stuff is gone. There's still plenty. Maybe not the fine antiques of 20 years ago, but who cares? If your breath catches in your throat when you see it, that's all that matters. I chose the markets in this book because they have the potential to make you gasp, and often, whether you are a devoted junker, vintage maven, or worshiper of antiques.

Some shows have been around for years and years like Brimfield, Massachusetts, with its traditional New England riches; or crazy-fun Round Top, Texas, where shows have martini bars and wealthy shoppers arrive by helicopter. Some are newer, like the shape-shifting Phila Flea that moves all over the city, and The Farm Chicks in Spokane that became an immediate sensation.

I've tried to include what you need to know to get there, eat well (or at least interestingly), find a place to sleep, and have a good time. So pick a show, pack your duds, visit the ATM, and get going.

⚡ what to take

You've seen all the rules and their variations: Take plenty of cash/take only as much as you can afford to spend. Don't carry a handbag/do carry a water bottle. Take a cart, hat, sweater, umbrella, boots, sunscreen, lip balm, toilet paper, tissues, and insect repellant. Nobody can do all that. Just decide what you need to be comfortable and carry on.

⚑ what to wear

Although a fisherman's vest with lots of pockets and covered with souvenir pins you bought at flea markets was the thing a while back, these are now seldom seen. Fashion is dictated by the particular market. Use your own style and add regional accents, like lumberjack plaids with flirty skirts in Minnesota. It's true that the Brooklyn Flea and Round Top are both considered super hip, but their styles are completely different. You will see few cowboy hats in Brooklyn, and few bow ties at Round Top. Boots are fine at either.

⚑ how to bargain

Bargaining is expected but don't insult the vendor by offering too little. Remember that on top of their purchase price, the vendor had to clean and perhaps repair or restyle the item, price it, haul it to the market, unload it, and display it. "What's your best price?" is always a nice way to start. Never offer less than half the asking price. If the price seems fair to me I often don't bargain at all.

⚑ most important

Don't worry about being the first one there. Use the porta-potties right after they've been cleaned. Have fun. I'll keep an eye out for you.

US Route 20
Brimfield, Massachusetts
Second week of May, July, and September
brimfield.com

brimfield antique show & flea market
brimfield, massachusetts

Brimfield is New England's Brigadoon. It appears three times a year along a short stretch of highway in eastern Massachusetts and for six delirious days promises to make your dreams come true. It's almost like being in love.

The market is made up of 21 different shows that open on staggered schedules from Tuesday through Sunday. Each has its own atmosphere, specialties, and fans. Overall, the market in May is the largest, July is the smallest, and September has the best bargains. There are thousands of dealers and 40,000 shoppers. The road is crowded with people hauling their treasures in carts or wagons; some speed by on bicycles or even roller skates. Traffic is awful. It's intimidating, confusing, difficult to navigate, and worth every minute spent there.

The market stretches only one linear mile but covers more than 100 acres. One way to tackle it is to divide it into three sections: east, central, and west. I like to browse one section, then move the car to the next, have a little sit-down, and resume shopping. This could take one day or five, however much time you care to spend. Some people take years to see it all.

Although shows advertise opening at daybreak, there's no need to arrive that early, especially later in the week when dealers sleep in. Start when it's comfortable. The exception is Tuesday, opening day, when, soon after the tent flaps go up, there's an electric scent of promise in the air that's very special. At that hour, it's quiet, easy to park, and there won't be a line for coffee. Seven-ish is a good time to get there.

⚑ day by day

MONDAY

One semi-secret is the spectacular one-day Vintage Fashion and Textile Show at the Host Hotel on Route 20 in Sturbridge. Many consider it the best textile show in the world. This is where ideas for next season's runway fashions originate. Early admission at 9:30 am is $20; general admission from 10:30 am to 5 pm is $10. Expect museum-quality period and designer clothing, workingman chic, bedcoverings, draperies, tapestries, sewing memorabilia, and estate jewelry. vintagefashionandtextileshow.com

TUESDAY

Opening day is always the most exciting, especially in May when dealers have been collecting all winter. Fifteen fields open at dawn. Park at the big white Congregational Church on the east end of Brimfield and cross Warren Road to Mahogany Ridge where the big tent on the corner always seems to have something irresistible in the way of turn-of-the-century furniture or artwork. It's tempting to buy large here because the car is so close. The first tent inside the field on the left is all vintage clothing with many hats, bags, and nightgowns.

Diagonally across the aisle (across from the breakfast stand) is a big tent housing several dealers with primitive kitchen tables, chairs, and everything needed to decorate a country kitchen, porch, or garden. From there it's easy to wander through four fields without ever looking up. At the empty field surrounded by a chain-link fence, cross the road and walk back through Central Park, which is a fine show with short aisles and is a nice place to slow down and breathe. The dealers here are old hands who've been showing for years, know what they have, and are gracious about sharing their knowledge and negotiating. The merchandise ranges from primitives to early 20th century.

If you want to continue, move the car to a central lot at Quaker Acres or to the adjoining field behind the chain-link fenced field where May's will open on Thursday (see Where to park, below). This is my favorite show. I get a cup of homemade chili at the stand in the back to renew strength and head toward the road where there is a huge tent offering transferware china, a glassware dealer, and a small group of dealers with early to mid-19th-century furniture and kitchen utensils.

An alternate plan is to begin at the far western end where two one-day shows open later in the day: Dealer's Choice, a big show with 400 dealers, opens at 11 am; Brimfield Acres North opens at 1 pm. Because these shows are so short, good dealers who don't have the time or desire to commit to a multiple-day show can be found here. They don't usually bother with tents, rather just set up tables and get ready to sell. The action on all sides is fast and furious; by late afternoon it's over. The diligent shopper can find good deals. There's parking in the nearby field. Lovers of postcards and paper will want to peek into the Ephemera Center on the grounds of Brimfield Acres North. It's open all week from 9 am to 6 pm.

WEDNESDAY

Three big shows open on Wednesday, but they will be there for the rest of the week so don't stress about getting to all in one day.

New England Motel opens at 6 am. There is a $5 admission fee for the first day only; after that it's free. On the north side of the street, it's easy to find by the food court that fronts the highway. Three covered pavilions house dealers with fine antiques, lighting, and vintage fashions.

Heart-O-the-Mart opens at 9 am. Avoid lines at the gate by arriving after 9:15 am. This show has a reputation for mid-century modern furniture as well as designer quality decorative accessories. It is home to the Textile Tent where some of the dealers from the Monday textile show do a reprise with their excellent antique quilts, rugs, and clothing dating back to the Civil War.

Hertan's opens at noon. Centrally located on the south side of the road, it's in a wide field shaded by mature trees, a treat in hot weather. It was founded in 1980 by Jeanne Hertan, the famous "lady in the white hat," who rang a big brass bell to announce the opening of every show. Known for excellent country, classical, and continental furniture and beautiful surprises, it's a favorite with designers and decorators and a place to spot celebrities.

THURSDAY

May's Antique Market opens at 9 am on the north side of the road next to Quaker Acres. Admission is $5. This inspired show draws big crowds and heavy traffic, so expect slow going into town. The entrance is on Route 20 with parking across the road but this lot is often filled long before nine. Fewer people use the rear entrance, accessible from Route 19 (see Where to park).

May's is a little frantic but worth it. The air is filled with the essence of a Colonial farmhouse and all it might include. You'll see lots of early cupboards and rainbows of milk paint. You may want to trim them with traditional stoneware jugs and silver servers, or offset them with arcane scientific instruments or a rusty tuba. For coal huggers, a dealer near the road has pristine cast-iron kitchen stoves. Porters are available in the center aisle.

FRIDAY

J & J Promotions, a two-day show, is open from 8 am to 4 pm on Friday and 9 am to 3 pm on Saturday. The field is on the south side of the road near the east end. There's plenty of parking. This one is the direct descendant of the original Brimfield show, then called Gordon Reid's Famous Flea Market. In

1959 auctioneer Reid, inspired by a flea market in Paris, assembled 100 dealers on his property for a little weekend sale. Daughters Jill and Judy, aka The Girls, grew up minding the booths and now run the show. Many still consider it the best. The field is spacious and grassy green with booths set in neat rows along little hillocks. It's pleasant, relaxed, and comfortable, offerings are tiptop and gloriously interesting.

SATURDAY AND SUNDAY

Shows remain open on Saturday; it can be crowded, but bargains start flying. Sunday is the unofficial bargain day, but many dealers have already left. Hint: Dealers who are headed south often set up on Sunday at The Elephant's Trunk Flea Market on Route 7 in New Milford, Connecticut, where they sell what they have left at very good prices.

⚑ brimfield rules
The show goes on, rain or shine, mud or flood; take boots in May. Early buying used to be the norm but is now universally prohibited. Parking is not permitted on roads and side streets; park in designated parking areas only (see Where to park). Don't be afraid to move the car, but remember where you parked it. Cell phone service is spotty because of high volume. It is not necessary to be first on the field. Porta-potties are a fact of life.

⚑ maps and information
The Brimfield Antique Guide is a free newspaper available at the show and throughout the area at shops, restaurants, and hotels. It has a map and lists all the shows with opening times.

⚑ carting and shipping
Many shows allow you to drive in and pick up purchases; some have porters who will take things to your car for a fee. For shipping, the Packaging Store has a booth on Route 20 at the May's parking lot. Their cell is (860) 729-0090 or call their store location at (888) 593-6683.

⚑ pets, etc.
Rules vary from field to field and some parking lots will not allow cars with pets inside. The management suggests shoppers not bring pets.

⚑ getting there
Brimfield is on US Route 20, 24 miles east of Springfield, Massachusetts, and 58 miles west of Boston. It is 161 miles from New York City. Traveling east on the

Mass Pike, take Exit 8 at Palmer to Route 20. It is six miles to Brimfield. Traveling west, exit at Route 20, Sturbridge, then go six miles to Brimfield. The GPS address is Brimfield Town Hall.

Brimfield partners with Pickup Pal, an eco-rideshare program. Sign up at pickuppal.com.

⚑ where to park

Parking is plentiful in the mornings but can be dicey later in the day. Look for signs at individual shows. There's no free parking. Charges range from $3 to $10 per lot. Best not to worry about the cost—it's convenient to be near the car in case of large purchases, forgotten necessities, or exhaustion. Don't park in the low-priced lots on the edge of town; they are too far away.

Two parking areas are recommended for their ease of access. The Congregational Church at the corner of Route 20 and Warren Road is a perfect place to park for browsing the markets at the east end, and the $10 fee helps support the church and its programs.

For central shows like Quaker Acres, May's, and Hertan's, avoid traffic by parking in the large field behind May's. To get there go a short distance north on Warren Road and turn left onto the dirt road after the Nathan Goodale B&B (red frame building). There's usually a flagman. The line of trees at the far end of the field borders the rear of Quaker Acres.

⚑ where to stay

Most people stay in Sturbridge where there are chain hotels, or at area inns and B&Bs. See brimfield.com for listings. Book early, especially for the May show.

⚔ where to eat

Many shows at the market have food concessions. It's always easy to find a breakfast sandwich, hot dog, or bowl of chili. For more choices, the food truck culture has arrived at Brimfield with New England specialties like lobster rolls, mini-potpies, pilgrim sandwiches (fresh roasted turkey, stuffing, and cranberries on a roll), even steamed lobsters. Look for trucks along the road near Central Park and in the food court at New England Motel.

Kaizen Sushi Bar and Grill

479 Main Street, Route 20, Sturbridge • (508) 347-1088 • kaizen479.com
Sunday to Tuesday 11:30 am to 9 pm; Wednesday to Saturday 11:30 am to 10 pm

After a long day on the fields one longs to clean up and have a quiet and relaxing dinner. The interior of Kaizen is meditative, the cocktails are chilled, and the sushi is some of the best in central Massachusetts.

Oxhead Tavern

336 Main Street (adjacent to the Host Hotel), Sturbridge • (508) 347-7393
sturbridgehosthotel.com • Monday to Thursday 11 am to 9 pm; Friday and Saturday 11 am to 10 pm; Sunday noon to 9 pm

This cozy New England-style tavern with a fireplace is set on a small lake with both a screened-in porch and a deck for summer dining.

The Duck

502 Main Street • (508) 347-2321 • theducksturbridge.com
Monday to Thursday 11:30 am to 9 pm; Friday and Saturday 11:30 am to 10 pm; Sunday 11:30 am to 8 pm

Dealers and shoppers mingle at the bar on the upper level of a Greek Revival building. The menu offers clam chowder, steaks, lobster mac and cheese, and other old-fashioned and updated pub food.

⚓ nearby attractions

Old Sturbridge Village

1 Old Sturbridge Village Road · (800) 733-1830 · osv.org
Wednesday to Sunday 9:30 am to 4 pm; closed Monday and Tuesday
Adults $24, seniors $22

If "junkers overload" sets in, retire to the 1830s and see all those antiques in actual use by costumed interpreters. Secret treat: there's an exhibit of clocks just inside the entrance gate. Be there on the hour or half-hour when all the chimes strike.

What I bought: at least seventy-five percent of the furnishings for the Tenement Museum in New York City, $85,000.

What I passed up: pale blue farmhouse table, $125.

What I will regret forever: polychrome bust of Renaissance noblewoman, $80.

summer market

176 Lafayette Avenue
(between Clermont and Vanderbilt Avenues)
Fort Greene, Brooklyn, New York
April to late November, rain or shine
Saturday, 10 am to 5 pm

East River State Park
(on the waterfront at North 7th Street)
Williamsburg, Brooklyn, New York
April to late November, rain or shine
Sunday, 10 am to 5 pm

winter market

Skylight One Hanson
1 Hanson Place (at Ashland Place)
Fort Greene, Brooklyn, New York
December through March
Saturday and Sunday, 10 am to 5 pm

brooklynflea.com

brooklyn flea
brooklyn, new york

Born in 2008, the Brooklyn Flea is an upstart in the world of venerable markets like Brimfield and Round Top, but what a cheeky little devil it is. It took about five minutes for it to become the must-go-to market in the country, and it's been topping the best flea markets lists in the blogs and magazines ever since.

It may not be for everyone; there aren't many classical antiques, and if it's fine silver it's probably a sweetly battered tea set. Things made before World War I are here, often for their odd/coolness factor. But for anything vintage or mid-century modern—original and refurbished furniture, color-saturated kitchenware, knick-knacks, art, lamps, fashion, past-season designer shoes, and Easter gloves—this is the place. There's handmade, too: Brooklyn kitchen towels, Brooklyn onesies, Brooklyn T-shirts, and plenty of jewelry in many forms.

The flea market is held every weekend year round with pretty much the same vendors, who are handpicked by the founders. In the warm months it's set up outdoors on two different sites. Every Saturday, it fills a schoolyard across from the Masonic Temple in Fort Greene. On Sunday, it sits on the edge of the East River in north Williamsburg with a grand view of Manhattan. Crowds gather to poke around, enjoy the sunshine, eat local food, and listen to live music.

In the winter you'll find it indoors at a raggedly ornate old bank building right off Flatbush Avenue. There are three floors of booths, on the balcony, under the sky-high windows on the main floor, and secreted away in basement vaults. Each dealer raises expectations for the next.

Those fond of the arcane should keep up with Old Croak as, with harrowing insight, they proffer items of great inherent beauty and connections to the past that would be the envy of the Victoria & Albert Museum. Be it in tatters or perfectly preserved, a checked Victorian bodice, gigantic light bulb, mercury glass owl, or ceremonial Masonic apron could assume top billing in any gently edgy living quarters.

With her snips and stitches, the Gifted Putterer is a must. A devoted collector of fragments, scraps, and remnants, our heroine shows up with canning jar sewing kits, boxes of jacquard ribbons, framed chromolithographs, handlettered gift tags, and trays full of tiny, mostly useless, objects that beg to be taken home.

The gentlemen owners of Hunters and Gatherers consider their booth a cabinet of curiosities. Veterans of visual display, they host a serene museum of animalia stocked with antlers, skulls, skins, shells, quills, and beetles under glass.

A play date at dAN's Parents' House should also be on the schedule. Dan Treiber grew up on City Island in the Bronx. A friend describes him as having "a sheer exuberance for crap." A few years back he bought his boyhood home from his

Red Hook

BLOCK NUMBERS ON THIS KEY
NOT CORRECTED. SEE DETAIL
SHEETS FOR CORRECT NUMBERS.

Vintage
Steel Body &
Aluminum
Beer Cans

dad. It was packed with stuff including tons of vintage toys, so he jumped right into the rummage business. He's at both fleas every weekend with piles of Star Wars figures, Smurfs, trolls, Simpsons memorabilia, Disney characters, games, cards, and so forth and so forth.

Indecision is not always fatal. Since many of the dealers set up at both locations, it's possible to pass something up on Saturday then find it again on Sunday. As the outdoor markets grow so does peripheral shopping. On Saturday stoop sales pop up in Fort Greene's classic brownstone neighborhoods. Sunday shoppers can wander off for more browsing along Bedford Avenue. And one mustn't forget that the Flea is regarded as New York City's top pick-up spot.

✠ pets, etc.

The flea welcomes pets whenever possible. They are allowed on Saturdays at Fort Greene, and on Sundays at Smorgasburg in DUMBO. Park rules prohibit them from the Sunday market at East River State Park in Williamsburg.

✠ getting there

Fort Greene
Subway: C to Lafayette Avenue; G to Clinton-Washington Avenue; B, D, N, Q, R, 2 ,3 ,4, 5 to Atlantic Avenue-Pacific Avenue

Williamsburg
Subway: L to Bedford Avenue, then walk west.
Ferry: East River Ferry to North 6th Street, North Williamsburg
Schedules at nywaterway.com

One Hanson Place Winter Market
Subway: C to Lafayette Avenue; G to Fulton Street; B, D, N, R, Q, 2, 3, 4, 5 to Atlantic Avenue/Barclays Center. The Atlantic Avenue stop is right across the street from One Hanson Place; follow the signs in the station.

✠ where to park

It is never easy or cheap to park in New York City. If possible, take the subway, the ferry, or a cab. Bikes are not ideal when carrying large purchases.

✠ where to stay

The Box House Hotel
77 Box Street, Greenpoint, Brooklyn • (718) 383-3800 • theboxhousehotel.com

Lodgings with kitchenettes, dishwashers, and big flat-screen TVs. Spaces range from 550-square-foot loft suites to 900-square-foot, two-bedroom lofts with terraces. Free transport in vintage checker cabs within one mile of the hotel.

⚑ where to eat

Smorgasburg

smorgasburg.com • Every weekend, April to mid-November, 11 am to 6 pm
Saturday: East River State Park, North 7th Street, Williamsburg
Sunday: Tobacco Warehouse, Brooklyn Bridge Park, near the intersection of Water and Dock Streets

There's plenty to eat at all three market locations, thanks to the flea's founders who pick the best from Brooklyn's huge food scene. Impressive as they are, the stands at the markets are mere satellites of the Flea's real culinary show, Smorgasburg, a gastrofest of glitzy street food that *The New York Times* called "The Woodstock of eating."

Smorgasburg keeps the same hours as the outdoor flea markets, but it's not in the same place. On Saturdays it occupies East River State Park where the Sunday flea takes place. On Sundays it's in DUMBO at Brooklyn Bridge Park in the Tobacco Warehouse. Choose from at least 100 pioneer chefs. It won't be easy with options like Bon Chovie's fried whole anchovies, crustacean delicacies from Red Hook Lobster Pound, fried chicken stuffed biscuits from Beehive Oven, Milk Truck grilled cheese sandwiches, Japanese/Mexican Takumi Tacos, chai-rhubarb popsicles from People's Pops, and oh so many others.

⚑ nearby attractions

Brooklyn Academy of Music

30 Lafayette Avenue, Fort Greene, Brooklyn

Flea markets and matinees aren't usually linked, but in Brooklyn it's possible to do just that. BAM's seven venues are only a few blocks from the Saturday and winter markets, and for the newest in dance, theater, music, films, art, and opera there's nothing quite like it. For full schedules and tickets see bam.org.

Brooklyn Bridge Park

On the East River under the Brooklyn Bridge

Come to munch at Smorgasburg in the shell of a Civil War era tobacco warehouse and stay to see the sites. The park is on the site where the Manhattan ferry docked in the 19th century. The area grew up then grew down as industrial grubbiness took away the river's appeal. It's still updating itself and now has 1.3 miles of riverfront with views, walks, a carousel, and former shipping piers that welcome dogs, swimmers, volleyball players, kids, and fishermen. Someone might be watching. In his 1856 poem "Crossing Brooklyn Ferry" Walt Whitman wrote,

"And you that shall cross from shore to shore years hence, are more to me, and more in my meditations, than you might suppose."

What I bought: nine ceramic Virgin Mary vases, $20.

What I passed up: large framed portrait of Kramer, price unknown.

What I will regret forever: bright yellow evening bag, $45.

P.S. 87
Columbus Avenue
(between West 76th and 77th Streets)
New York, New York

April to October
Sunday, 10 am to 5:45 pm

November to March
Sunday, 10 am to 5:30 pm

greenfleamarkets.com

greenflea
new york, new york

Every Sunday morning, Columbus Avenue behind the American Museum of Natural History becomes a promenade of amblers, browsers, brunchers, and lovers, as the Upper West Side presents its version of Portobello Road. This is mostly because of GreenFlea, Manhattan's biggest flea market. It's held in the schoolyard of Public School 87, where those who still long for recess can look forward to some serious grown-up playtime.

The market is owned by the school's Parents Association, and has been around since 1985 when it was founded by a mom who envisioned a nice income stream for the school. Since then the market has contributed an amazing four million dollars, which has been used to enrich the school's programs. In exchange for giving up their playground on Sundays, P.S. 87 kids get art, music, dance, and yoga classes. Not a bad trade.

GreenFlea is probably the best flea market in the city for higher-end antiques, vintage designer clothing, and estate jewelry. Just take a look at the sumptuous fur coats near the Columbus Avenue gate. Many dealers have been selling here for years and have an established clientele who depend on them when they need a little style pick-up. From Deco draperies to French tablecloths to Louis chairs, this market always comes through.

An unusual vendor who shows here regularly is Scott Jordan, digger of history, who has been collecting old bottles, brushless toothbrushes, clay pipes, and shards of pottery from New York City privy pits, wells, and construction sites for more than 40 years. The objects he finds become material for his art, which includes collage, painting, and jewelry. His necklaces made of bits of broken dishes set with jewels, beads, and chains are exquisite souvenirs of bygone New York.

Another interesting booth deals in ethnographic art and collectible seashells. On one side, glass cases are filled with pocket-sized cultural curiosities from Africa, Indonesia, the Philippines, and the American Southwest. On the other, stark white starfish and sand dollars tumble over brilliantly colored whelks, clams, and an occasional nautilus.

A sizeable contingent of artisans brings handmade items: knitted scarves and mitts, industrial jewelry, sheerly lovely little dresses, handbags, and greeting cards. And there is no lack of clothing both vintage and new, from outerwear to underwear, leather jackets to plastic rain boots.

The market continues inside the school. This section is a bit cozier in cold or wet weather. The most valuable small antiques, estate jewelry, and silver are in the cafeteria.

Nikki Stark of Jewelbiz, on the right as you walk in the cafeteria door, has been with GreenFlea for thirty years. Hers is the longest tenure of any dealer.

Her specialty is brooches for both women and men. She is next to the teacup ladies whose sweetly decorated Victorian-era cups hail from England, France, and Japan. Remember that Victoria was queen for a long time, 1837 to 1901, so that includes a lot of teacups.

Just down the aisle, Maya Schaper has deeply interesting 19th- and early 20th-century pieces for ordinary use and with extraordinary design, such as early ice cream scoops, brass handheld scales, and school bells.

GreenFlea also has a farmers market, which is set up along Columbus Avenue under the giant plane trees behind the natural history museum. There are vendors of all the usual produce: fresh corn-on-the-cob, melons, beans, apples, tons of heirloom tomatoes. More unusual stands include the mushroom guy, a fishmonger, the ostrich man, the cheese damsels, several bakers, and the lavender tent.

Twice a year in April and October, Crafts on Columbus takes over the greenmarket space with a major designer market. Everything from fine handmade sterling silver jewelry to mischievous hand-knitted hats draws big crowds. When Crafts on Columbus is in session, the greenmarket moves across the street adjacent to and in the rear schoolyard of P.S. 87.

⌑ pets, etc.
Pets are not permitted.

⌑ getting there
B or C subway to 81st Street-Museum of Natural History, or 1 subway to 79th Street. Check service advisories; the MTA not infrequently shuts down train

lines on weekends for repairs. The free app iTrans NYC is helpful. Or, catch the M10 bus on Central Park West, the M11 down Columbus Avenue, or the M79 crosstown.

⚓ where to park

If you can find on-street parking, you get a gold star for extreme gumption. There are a few garages, but they are not close and the cost will seriously deplete your mad money.

⚓ where to stay

The Excelsior Hotel
45 West 81st Street (between Central Park West and Columbus Avenue)
(212) 362-9200 • excelsiorhotelny.com

Newly renovated, popular, and also home to Calle Ocho Restaurant, famous for its Latin fusion food and a glittery young clientele. (212) 873-5025, calleochonyc.com

⚓ where to eat

There's pick-up food just inside the 77th Street gates where a gathering of vendors sells savory quiches, Greek pastries, soup, and pickles. For a sit-down meal the neighborhood is full of restaurants.

Isabella's
359 Columbus Avenue at West 77th Street • (212) 724-2100 • isabellas.com
Monday to Thursday 11:30 am to 10 pm; Friday 11:30 am to 11 pm;
Saturday 10 am to 11 pm; Sunday 10 am to 10 pm

This is a top stop for brunch, pasta, and people watching with plentiful outdoor seating.

Ocean Grill

384 Columbus Avenue at West 78th Street • (212) 579-2300 • oceangrill.com

Monday to Thursday 11:30 am to 10:30 pm; Friday 11:30 am to 11 pm;
Saturday 11:30 am to 11:30 pm; Sunday 10:30 am to 10:30 pm

Very fresh seafood is the specialty here at one of Manhattan's standbys.

Shake Shack

366 Columbus Avenue at West 77th Street • (646) 747-8770 • shakeshack.com

Daily 10:45 am to 11 pm

Inexpensive top-quality burgers, hot dogs, shakes, and frozen custard—and a short (two-item) menu for dogs. Great for kids.

⚓ nearby attractions

American Museum of Natural History
Central Park West (between West 77th and West 81st Streets)
(212) 769-5100 • amnh.org • Daily 10 am to 5:45 pm

One of the world's grandest museums, it occupies a 17-acre park with 25 interconnecting buildings and has 32 million specimens. If your eye is still focused on antiques, the meticulous old dioramas are worth a visit, especially the Akeley Hall of African Mammals that was opened in 1936. The Columbus Avenue entrance is closest to the flea market and is open in the summer months. Main entrances are on 81st Street at the bright blue Rose Science Center, and on Central Park West where you can see very big dinosaur skeletons.

New York Historical Society
170 Central Park West at West 77th Street • (212) 873-3400 • nyhistory.org
Tuesday to Thursday, Friday 10 am to 8 pm; Saturday 10 am to 6 pm;
Sunday 11 am to 5 pm; closed Monday

Newly revamped, bright and airy, the historical society has made its fourth floor into a wonderland for lovers of antiques, where nearly 40,000 objects from the collections are on permanent display at the Luce Center for the Study of American Culture. The entrance on West 77th Street near Central Park West also accesses the excellent museum shop and Caffé Storico, a lovely place to dine beneath golden chandeliers and walls lined with shelves of white china. Tuesday to Sunday 11 am to 10 pm; brunch Saturday and Sunday 11 am to 3 pm; closed Monday.

Central Park
Central Park West (one block east of the flea market) • Entrances at West 81st Street, West 77th Street, and West 72nd Street • centralparknyc.org

Beautiful in any season: watch kids fly kites on the Great Lawn, listen to itinerant musicians, rent a rowboat, or just find a nice place to sit down.

What I bought: Black velvet swing coat. $7.

What I passed up: Louis chair upholstered with peacock fabric, $450.

What I will regret forever: Pendant necklace made from a 19th-century Frozen Charlotte doll that was found in a privy pit. $95.

45

winter
Spring Garden Indoor Antique &
Vintage Market
820 Spring Garden Street (at 9th Street)
Philadelphia, Pennsylvania
November through March
1st and 3rd Saturdays
8 am to 4 pm

spring and fall
Broad and Callowhill,
Fairmount,
Head House Square Antique &
Vintage Market,
Jefferson Square Park,
Kimmel Center for the Performing Arts,
Main Street-Manayunk,
Old City-2nd and Arch,
Passyunk Avenue at Morris Street,
Sister Cities Park,
Society Hill,
South Street

April through October
Saturday, 9 am to 5 pm
(8 am to 4 pm in late fall)

philafleamarkets.org

phila flea markets
philadelphia, pennsylvania

The elusive Phila Flea keeps devotees guessing as it leapfrogs around town to eight, nine, eleven different locations and entwines itself with art openings, neighborhood barbeques, jugglers, street bands, fortune tellers, bake sales, a basilica, a prison museum, and a church attended by George Washington. Only in the winter does it settle down and become the Spring Garden Indoor Antique & Vintage Market.

Each location hosts two markets each year, one in the spring and one in the fall. All are on Saturday except for the First Friday Market. The usual time is 9 am to 5 pm. As days get shorter in the fall, hours change to 8 am to 4 pm. The full schedule is at philafleamarkets.org.

This may sound convoluted but is actually lots of fun. Philadelphia has distinctive neighborhoods and each one provides a new backdrop. Locals get an excuse to visit other parts of town and out-of-towners discover an itinerary that wouldn't appear in any guidebook. A good example is the weekend when the artsy First

Friday Flea is followed on Saturday by the home-grown Fairmount Flea.

Old City happens in conjunction with First Friday art nights in Philadelphia's most historic neighborhood. The flea is on 2nd Street at Arch Street and runs north toward the Ben Franklin Bridge and south toward Market Street. Dealers set up against old industrial buildings and in a parking lot at the end of Elfreth's Alley, the oldest surviving residential street in the country.

The sidewalks are narrow here, so there isn't much furniture, but plenty of vintage, very good buys on jewelry, art, and a surprising number of religious articles. Artists join in, selling drawings and small paintings. As it gets dark, dealers start to pack up. Their places are taken by street musicians (one old guy was playing "Hey Jude" on the fiddle), gallery goers, and the bar crowd, as the party continues.

The next morning some of the same dealers and many others set up across town, along the twenty-foot-high stone walls of Eastern State Penitentiary. This melancholy landmark was opened in 1829 and is now a museum. A lovely garden planted by the Pennsylvania Horticultural Society tempers the east and south sides of the prison. Dealers display antiques on a low wall surrounding it, so don't be surprised to see teakettles emerging from rudbeckia or statues of saints among the roses. The neighborhood comes out to celebrate with corner barbeques and little stands selling homemade baked goods.

⚓ pets, etc.

The outdoor markets are on public sidewalks and in public parks so dogs on leashes should be fine. Neighborhood rules apply.

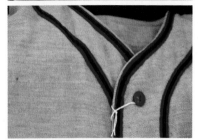

⚓ getting there

Driving in Philadelphia is fairly easy, as is walking. New Yorkers can take an easy Amtrak ride from dreary Penn Station to luminous 30th Street Station in West Philadelphia. All the fleas are a short taxi or subway ride away.

⚓ where to park

It's often possible to park on the street. Parking is also available in garages like those operated by Central Parking. Their website has all the locations with rates, plus printable discount coupons and a free app for searching while on the go. philadelphia.centralparking.com

⚓ byob

In Philadelphia it is super cool to Bring Your Own Bottle. More than 200 restaurants have joined the BYOB craze that allows small restaurant owners to save money by not buying a liquor license and diners to lower the cost of dining out. Some restaurants charge corking fees and some don't.

⚓ additional markets

Whether by design or by accident many of the markets are located near historic sites, or perhaps all of Philadelphia is a historic site. In any case, there are currently eleven markets, but the number will probably continue to grow. The markets below are presented as mini-breaks with places to stay, restaurants, and things to see. For more good places to stay and eat see Philadelphia Neighborhoods at visitphilly.com.

Broad & Callowhill

1400 Callowhill Street • See philafleamarkets.org for date and time.

The Callowhill neighborhood is generally known as the Loft District because of its industrial character, but insiders call it the Eraserhood in honor of film director David Lynch who lived there while in college and used it as inspiration for his cult classic *Eraserhead*. It's an art/music destination where the polite bistros of Center City give way to workingmen's bars and rockabilly, psychobilly, and Nancy Sinatra.

The market is easy to find. Just search the skyline for the white clock tower of the former *Philadelphia Enquirer* building. Across the street in a parking lot, vendors will be selling funky-punky vintage and unexpected treasures.

⚑ where to park

There's street parking on Callowhill, Broad, and Wood Streets and at a surface lot at the southeast corner of Broad and Callowhill.

Subway: Take the Broadway Street subway to the Race/Vine stop.

⚑ where to stay

This market is shouting distance from City Hall and the Convention Center which are surrounded by chain hotels. A couple of close ones are the Hilton Garden Inn on Arch Street and the Holiday Inn Express on Walnut Street.

⚑ where to eat

Cafe Lift
428 North 13th Street • (215) 922-3031
Tuesday to Sunday 9 am to 3 pm

PENNSYLVANIA SOCIETY
SONS OF THE REVOLUTION
PROCEEDINGS
1929-1933

Brunch and good coffee are served at Cafe Lift, one block east on 13th Street, which is getting sweeter every day. Cash only.

Prohibition Taproom
501 North 13th Street • (215) 238-1818
Monday to Friday 4 pm to 2 am; Saturday and Sunday 11 am to 2 am.

If the time for brunch has passed, walk one more block for beautiful beer and homemade kielbasa and pierogies.

⚓ nearby attractions

The Trestle Inn
11th and Callowhill Streets • (267) 239-0290 • thetrestleinn.com
Daily 5 pm to 2 am; happy hour Monday to Friday 5 pm to 7 pm

More than one hundred years old and still raging, The Trestle Inn brags about infinite brands of whiskey, retro cocktails, go-go dancers, and mean deviled eggs. Music usually starts at 10 pm. See the website for schedules.

Fairmount

22nd Street and Fairmount Avenue • See philafleamarkets.org for date and time.

Called by some "The Prison Flea," because it circles the penitentiary, this market is an impressive mix of old and newer goods at all prices, augmented by picturesque views and dealer laissez-faire. Proceeds benefit the Fairmount Community Development Corporation and the Friends of Eastern State Penitentiary Park.

⚲ where to park

A public lot is on the northwest corner of 22nd Street and Fairmount Avenue.

⚲ where to stay

Best Western Center City

501 North 22nd Street • (215) 568-8300 • book.bestwestern.com

This hotel is not particularly picturesque but it's only a few blocks from the flea market, next door to the Barnes Foundation and the Rodin Museum, and easy walking distance to the Philadelphia Museum of Art. The rates are flea friendly, the pool is big, it allows pets, and it offers free parking, a rarity in this part of the city.

The Latham Hotel

135 South 17th Street • (215) 563-7474 • lathamhotelphiladelphia.com

For fancier digs at a fancier price, the Latham near Rittenhouse Square is an historic boutique hotel with lovely décor and a nice restaurant. It, too, allows pets.

The Windsor Suites • see page 68

⚓ where to eat

Jack's Firehouse

2130 Fairmount Avenue • (215) 232-9000 • jacksfirehouse.com
Monday to Friday 11:30 am to 10:30 pm; Saturday 11 am to 10:30 pm;
Sunday 11 am to 9pm

In an 1870s firehouse 100 feet from the main entrance of the prison, Jack's Firehouse is so close that flea marketers can break for refreshments then get right back to shopping. Brunch Saturday and Sunday 11 am to 3 pm, then choose from the bar menu.

⚓ nearby attractions

Eastern State Penitentiary

2027 Fairmount Avenue • (215) 236-3300 • easternstate.org
Daily 10 am to 5 pm (last admission 4 pm)

Opened in 1829, this is the oldest penitentiary in America. After a visit in 1842 Charles Dickens wrote, "The system here is rigid, strict, and hopeless solitary confinement. I believe it, in its effects, to be cruel and wrong." The prison is now a vast museum. Visitors are allowed to ramble alone through "a lost world of crumbling cellblocks and empty guard towers."

Inmate Freda H. Frost must have channeled the flea market on her way in. Upon her arrival in 1913 to begin a 20-year sentence for poisoning her husband she carried three bracelets, two earrings, eight rings, one watch and chain, 11 spoons, two cuff buttons, two charms, a breast pin, and a locket missing a stone.

Headhouse Square Antique & Vintage Market
2nd Street between Pine and Lombard Streets
See philafleamarkets.org for date and time.

Headhouse Square is Philadelphia's oldest outdoor market. The square and market buildings are a colonial delight. A headhouse is a firehouse, and this one has been here since 1803, making it the oldest in America. Originally there were two, one on either end of a long open-sided colonnade called the Shambles where merchants have been setting out their wares for over 200 years. There's a farmers market every Sunday, a crafts show in the summertime, and our friend the flea in autumn and spring. Only antiques and vintage merchandise of prime quality are sold here.

⚓ where to park
A parking garage is at 2nd and Lombard Streets, there is also parking directly south of the market between Lombard and South Streets.

⚓ where to stay
Sheraton Philadelphia Society Hill Hotel
One Dock Street · (215) 238-6000 · sheraton.com/societyhill

Easy walking to both Society Hill and Headhouse Square Markets. With river views and posh linens, this feels like a boutique hotel.

⚲ where to eat

Cavanaugh's Headhouse Square

421 South 2nd Street • (215) 928-9307 • cavsheadhouse.com

Monday to Thursday 2:30 pm to 2 am; Friday 11:30 am to 2 am;
Saturday and Sunday 9:30 am to 2 am

Pub food in a late 18th-century tavern, served with devotion to European sports like rugby and cricket.

⚲ nearby attractions

A Man Full of Trouble Tavern

127 Spruce Street • Private residence

Sources suggest there were 120 taverns in Philadelphia before the Revolutionary War; this is the only one left standing. Its odd name is typical of colonial tavern nomenclature; indeed, its original name is thought to have been The Man Loaded With Mischief. Unfortunately one can no longer get a pint of ale here. After falling into great disrepair the building was purchased by the University of Pennsylvania, shored up, and is now a private residence for two historians who care for the property.

Jefferson Square Park Antique and Vintage Market

Washington Avenue between 3rd and 4th Streets in Pennsport section of South Philadelphia • See philafleamarkets.org for date and time.

This flea is set in an early 19th-century park near what was once the ship-building center of Philadelphia, an area that has seen Civil War encampments, urban decay, and most recently, renovation. About 125 vendors bring mainly vintage merchandise. Proceeds benefit the Friends of Jefferson Square Park.

⚑ where to park
Park on the street.

⚑ where to stay
Sheraton Philadelphia Society Hill Hotel · see page 58

⚑ where to eat
Federal Donuts
1219 South 2nd Street · (267) 687-8258 · federaldonuts.com
Monday to Friday 7 am to 3 pm, Saturday and Sunday 7 am to 6 pm or
until the donuts are gone.

Serves coffee, donuts, and fried chicken only, to boundless popular acclaim.

⚑ nearby attractions
The Mummer's Museum
1100 South 2nd Street · (215) 336-3050 · mummersmuseum.com
Wednesday to Saturday 9:30 am to 4:30 pm

Mummers have been marching through the streets of Philadelphia every
New Year's Day since the mid-19th century. All-male groups of singing and
dancing revelers, they wear spectacular feathered-spangled-beaded costumes
that can cost tens of thousands of dollars to construct. The Mummers Museum
displays prize-winning costumes from past years, some dating back to the early
20th century.

Kimmel Center for the Performing Arts

300 South Broad Street at Spruce Street • See philafleamarkets.org for date and time.

Home of the Philadelphia Orchestra, Opera Philadelphia, and PHILADANCO among others, this air-conditioned arts center is the only indoor venue during the summer season. Vendors will be showing top-drawer antiques and fine vintage merchandise as befits the luxe setting.

⚑ where to park

The Kimmel has a parking garage with an entrance on Broad Street.

Subway: Take the Broad Street Subway to the Walnut-Locust stop.

⚑ where to stay

The Independent Hotel

1234 Locust Streeet • (215) 772-1440 • theindependenthotel.com.

A calm and restorative boutique hotel a few blocks from the Kimmel Center. Amenities include rooms with fireplaces, and architectural features like exposed brick and cathedral ceilings.

The Latham • see page 57

Alexander Inn

12th and Spruce Streets • (215) 923-3535 • alexanderinn.com.

The Alexander was built as an apartment building in the early 20th century. It has evolved into a boutique hotel whose many fans wish that its existence would remain a secret. So don't tell anyone, just try to snag a reservation.

✠ where to eat

Amis

412 South 13th Street at Waverly • (215) 732-2647 • amisphilly.com
Sunday to Thursday 5 pm to 10 pm; Friday and Saturday 5 pm to 11 pm;
Sunday brunch 10 am to 2 pm

Cacio e pepe like they make it in Rome. Amis doesn't serve lunch but it's worth waiting around until they open at 5 pm. Sunday brunch is a triumphant hybrid of an American breakfast and a long afternoon meal in an Umbrian garden.

Bob and Barbara's

1509 South Street near 15th Street • (215) 545-4511 • bobandbarbaras.com
Monday to Friday 3 pm to 2 am; Saturday 11 am to 2 am; Sunday noon to 2 am

Bob and Barbara's is Philly's favorite dive bar, and the birthplace of Philly's favorite drink. It is an accepted fact that "The Special," a can of Pabst Blue Ribbon beer and a shot of Jim Beam, originated here in 1994. All sorts of people hang here, play ping-pong, listen to live music, watch drag shows, and just have a good time. It's not fancy. Come as you are.

✠ nearby attractions

See a show at the Kimmel. Schedules and tickets are at kimmelcenter.org.

Main Street–Manayunk

4200 block of Main Street at Pensdale Street in Manayunk
See philafleamarkets.org for date and time.

Manayunk is an old canal town on the Schuylkill River in northwest Philadelphia that is now a center for shopping and nightlife. Hilly and picturesque, with small rowhouses and lots of churches, it's on the National Register of Historic Places. The name comes from the Lenape Indian word for "place to drink," appropriate since it's filled with bars and restaurants. With its history and numerous home furnishings stores and boutiques, it's an obvious location for the flea market, which is located in three parking lots on Main Street.

⚓ where to park

Public parking lots are located at Shurs Lane near Main Street, west of Main Street at Locke Street, Cresson and Cotton Streets, Main Street at Levering Street, Green Lane; revenue supports city infrastructure. On-street parking is also available.

⚓ where to stay

Manayunk Terrace Bed & Breakfast

3937 Terrace Street • (215) 483-0109 • manayunkterrace.com

Called by its owner "the petite hotel," this B&B has all the luxuries like Wi-Fi, Jacuzzis, steam baths, and flat-screen televisions, plus a roof deck and an elevator.

⚓ where to eat

The Couch Tomato Café and The Tomato Bistro

102 Rector Street • (215) 483-2233 • manayunktomato.com
Sunday to Thursday 11 am to 10 pm; Friday and Saturday 11 am to 11 pm

The Café is downstairs and casual; The Bistro is directly upstairs and a little fancier. Together they are rated tops in Philly and are worshipped for their fresh soups, salads, panini, wraps, and pizza; vegetarian and vegan are no problem.

⚓ nearby attractions

Schuylkill River Trail

access at Locke Street west of Main Street • schuylkillrivertrail.com

Just steps from the flea market, the trail follows the towpath of the Manayunk Canal through a landscape of 19th-century industrial buildings and bridges. The trailhead is on Locke Street; parking is on the opposite side of the canal.

Old City

2nd Street and Arch Street • First Friday of the month, 5 pm to 9 pm

Dealers set up along the sidewalk for several blocks, near the Ben Franklin Bridge, in what is known as "the most historic square mile in America." This location is near many historic sites, restaurants, and hotels. See oldcitydistrict.org.

⚓ where to park

Park on Arch Street between 2nd and 3rd Streets, or in a $5 lot at 41 North 6th Street (good for all night). Parking meters are free on First Fridays.

⚓ where to stay

There are many chain hotels with various rates near Independence Mall. For something a little different see below.

Penn's View Hotel

14 North Front Street at Market Street • (215) 922-7600 • pennsviewhotel.com

This boutique hotel on the Delaware River has grand views and is close to the historic center. The décor is a bit over the top, but antique lovers won't mind.

Monaco Philadelphia, a Kimpton Hotel
433 Chestnut Street • (216) 925-2111 • monaco-philadelphia.com
The Monaco caresses Independence Mall, is considered the best in town, and is wildly gorgeous. A room can be had for $300+ per night.

⚑ where to eat

Chloe
232 Arch Street • (215) 629-2337 • chloebyob.com
Wednesday through Saturday 5 pm to 9:30 pm; closed Sunday to Tuesday

One block west of the market, Chloe serves fresh food in a cozy setting—pizza with fig jam and gorgonzola, baby back ribs, braised fennel with mozzarella and pine nuts, and much more. No reservations are taken. BYOB.

⚑ nearby attractions

Betsy Ross House
239 Arch Street • (215) 686-1252 • betsyrosshouse.org
December to February, Tuesday to Sunday 10 am to 5 pm;
March to November, daily 10 am to 5 pm

A costumed interpreter portrays the famous flag designer at work in her little shop.

Christ Church & Christ Church Burial Ground
Second Street just north of Market Street • (215) 922-1695 • christchurchphila.org
Church: Monday to Saturday 9 am to 5 pm; Sunday 1 pm to 5 pm
Burial ground: Monday to Saturday 10 am to 4 pm; Sunday noon to 4 pm

Known as "The Nation's Church," founded 1695. Benjamin Franklin is buried here.

The Museum of Elfreth's Alley

124 Elfreth's Alley • (215) 574-0560 • elfrethsalley.org
Guided tours January to March, Thursday to Sunday 11 am to 5 pm; April to December, Tuesday to Saturday 10 am to 5 pm (last tour leaves 40 minutes before closing)

The 32 houses on this picturesque street were constructed between 1728 and 1836. Two homes are open to the public. Tours begin at the Museum, number 124.

Passyunk Avenue at Morris Street

1600 block of Passyunk Avenue between Tasker and Morris Streets, South Philadelphia • See philafleamarkets.org for date and time

Sometimes just called "the Avenue," or sometimes "P'unk," or sometimes "Pashyunk," this old Italian neighborhood is where the Philly cheesesteak was invented. Now mom-and-pop *ristoranti* are scattered among Wi-Fi cafés and vegan grocery stores on what is called "the hottest strip in Philadelphia," certainly a good place for a flea market. There's the regular vintage and jewelry, but the taste of the shoppers here prompts some dealers to bring the slightly peculiar and decidedly weird, often for the better.

⚑ where to park

There is free two-hour parking on side streets, metered parking on the Avenue, and a parking garage on the corner of Broad and McKean Streets.

⚑ where to stay

Alexander Inn • see page 61

⚑ where to eat

Capogiro Gelataria

1625 East Passyunk Avenue • (215) 462-3790 • capogirogelato.com

Summer hours: Daily 10 am to 10 pm

Old-fashioned Italian desserts are trumped by transformative Capogiro gelato in flavors like Madagascar Bourbon Vanilla and Ricotta with Sliced Almonds.

⚑ nearby attractions

The Mütter Museum

19 South 22nd Street at the College of Physicians • (215) 563-3737

collegeofphysicians.org • Daily 10 am to 5 pm

Not nearby, but those with a yen for the bizarre will enjoy the oddities at this museum of medical specimens.

Sister Cities Park

Benjamin Franklin Parkway at 18th Street

See philafleamarkets.org for date and time.

Antiques and vintage goods are the order of the day when the market moves into Sister Cities Park on the east side of Logan Square. It couldn't be in a prettier place, in this newish park between the splashing of Logan Square Fountain and the majesty of the Basilica of Saints Peter and Paul. Even those who care not for fleas will have plenty to see and do.

⚑ where to park

On-street parking is available nearby.

⚓ where to stay

The Windsor Suites

1700 Benjamin Franklin Parkway at 17th Street • (215) 981-5678
thewindsorsuites.com

The Windsor is only a short block from the market and is a good value. All the rooms are suites with fully equipped kitchens, from studios to one bedroom, or even larger. There are even unfurnished apartments available in case your flea market shopping gets out of hand. Parking is extra.

Best Western Center City • see page 56

⚓ where to eat

Milk & Honey Café

200 North 18th Street in Sister Cities Park • (215) 665-8600
milkandhoneymarket.com • Monday to Friday 7 am to 6 pm; Thursday until 7 pm; Saturday and Sunday 8 am to 5 pm

Breakfast is served all day at this café adjoining the market. Fresh local bagels, breakfast sandwiches, soup of the day, panini, cupcakes, brownies, and cookies are all made with the freshest ingredients. There's a kids' menu, too.

Kite & Key

1836 Callowhill Street • (215) 568-1818 • thekiteandkey.com
Kitchen hours: Sunday to Tuesday 11 am to 11 pm; Wednesday 11 am to midnight; Thursday to Saturday 11 am to 1 am; bar open daily until 2 am.

Nearby, updated pub food and a large selection of beer is served inside or outdoors. Casual. The name comes from Benjamin Franklin's experiments with electricity.

⚓ nearby attractions

Cathedral Basilica of Saints Peter and Paul

1723 Race Street • (215) 561-1313 • cathedralphila.org
Monday to Friday 7:30 am to 4:30 pm; Saturday 9 am to 5:15 pm;
Sunday 8 am to 6:30 pm

That gorgeous church across the street is the Basilica of Saints Peter and Paul. It is the mother church of the Archdiocese of Philadelphia. Modeled after San Carlo al Corso in Rome, it was opened in 1864 when the Civil War was still going on and Abraham Lincoln was president. Visitors are welcomed all day; Cathedral Ambassadors answer questions and give mini-tours. There are no Caravaggios but the art and architecture are comparable to that found in many renowned European churches. For detailed history see the website.

Society Hill

3rd and Pine Streets surrounding St. Peter's Church & School, entrance on Lombard Street • See philafleamarkets.org for date and time.

This market is one block from Headhouse Square and winds its way around St. Peter's Church, which opened in 1761 and has been holding services ever since. George and Martha Washington often worshipped there and why wouldn't they, the interior is gorgeous. It's a fixture of Society Hill, named not for the socialites assumed to have lived there, but for the Free Society of Traders, a company of wealthy Englishmen who backed William Penn in his effort to make Philadelphia a commercial success. The 75 or so dealers here are also hoping for commercial success and bring lovely and interesting things.

⚑ where to park

There is free parking in the St. Peter's schoolyard.

⚑ where to stay

Sheraton Philadelphia Society Hill Hotel • see page 58

⚑ where to eat

Pizzeria Stella

2nd and Lombard Streets • (215) 320-8000 • pizzeriastella.net

Monday to Thursday 11:30 am to 10 pm; Friday 11:30 am to 11 pm;
Saturday 11 am to 11 pm; Sunday 11 am to 10 pm

Although best-known for pizza, the menu includes antipasti, soup, salads, and pasta.

⚑ nearby attractions

Churchyard of St. Peter's Church

313 Pine Street

A stroll in a cemetery is always relaxing and this one is a quiet oasis of grass and gravestones. Remarkable residents include Colonel John Nixon, who gave the first public reading of the Declaration of Independence four days after it was signed; painter Charles Willson Peale, first portraitist of George Washington; George Mifflin Dallas, vice president under James K. Polk, who had a town in Texas named after him; and the chiefs of seven indigenous tribes who died of smallpox on a visit to Philadelphia in 1793.

South Street

Circles the block between 10th Street and 11th Street from South Street north to Lombard Street • See philafleamarkets.org for date and time.

South Street was Philadelphia's Haight Ashbury. It has always been dodgy; in colonial times it was purposely zoned outside the city limits because of its reputation as a hangout for crooks and pirates. In the late 1940s city planners, led by Edmund Bacon, Kevin Bacon's dad, broached the idea of turning it into a crosstown expressway, which led to 25 years of haggling and the resulting decay. By the mid-1960s it was little more than empty buildings, garbage, and ultra-cheap rents. Just the place to settle if you were young, broke, and a hippie.

The first hippies to move in were Isaiah and Julia Zagar, newly returned from the Peace Corps in Peru and toting crates of handmade goods from the Andes. In 1968 they opened a shop called Eyes Gallery, which is still in its original building at 402 South Street. Julia says, "By 1974, all the old people were gone and it really was a hippie village. We had a Hippie House Tour in response to the Society Hill house tours."

Eventually the expressway was defeated, more and more people moved in, then the chain stores—and that was the end of the South Street strip. But every few months a bit of the free spirited past returns when the flea market comes to town. Dealers (surely some are old hippies), set up along South Street and around Seger Park Playground in a casual disarray of tables, blankets, vans, and car trunks. There are plenty of souvenirs from the halcyon hippie days, but now they're called vintage and everyone wants them. Proceeds benefit the Friends of Seger Park Playground.

⚓ where to park

Central Parking garage on South Street between 10th and 11th Streets; enter at South 11th and Rodman Streets. On-street parking is also available.

⚓ where to stay

Alexander Inn • see page 61

⚓ where to eat

Supper

926 South Street • (215) 592-8180 • supperphilly.com
Monday 5:30 pm to 9 pm; Tuesday to Thursday 5:30 pm to 11 pm;
Friday 5:30 pm to 11:30 pm; Saturday 10:30 am to 3 pm (brunch), 5:30 pm to 11:30 pm; Sunday 10:30 am to 3 pm (brunch), 5:30 pm to 9 pm

Weekend brunch features red velvet waffles and gingerbread pancakes, not to mention biscuits, grits, and deviled eggs, all served in Supper's "urban farmhouse."

Reading Terminal Market

51 North 12th Street at Arch Street • (215) 922-2317 • readingterminalmarket.org
General vendors: Monday to Saturday 8 am to 6 pm; Sunday 9 am to 5pm
Pennsylvania Dutch vendors: Tuesday and Wednesday 8 am to 3 pm;
Thursday to Saturday 8 am to 5pm; closed Sunday

This is the food court of your dreams, with specialties from hot, handmade pretzels to oysters on the half-shell. There are seating areas but think quick to grab a seat. It is rated one of the top eating establishments in the city and is a real trip.

✠ nearby attractions

Philadelphia's Magic Gardens

1020 South Street • (215) 733-0390 • phillymagicgardens.org
Summer: Sunday to Thursday 11 am to 6 pm, Friday and Saturday 11 am to
8 pm; Winter: Sunday to Thursday 11 am to 5 pm, Friday and Saturday 11 am
to 8 pm

The fantastical mosaic-covered architecture and sculptures of the visionary
artist and South Street pioneer Isaiah Zagar, are open daily and include an
outdoor sculpture garden and an indoor grotto of tunnels, shards, and mirrors.

Spring Garden Indoor Antique & Vintage Market

Southeast corner 9th Street and Spring Garden Street
Every 1st and 3rd Saturday from November through March, 8 am to 4 pm

In winter the market centralizes inside a 36,000-square-foot ground-floor warehouse with heat, a food court, and an ATM. All the dealers take advantage of
the hospitable atmosphere and bring really good furniture, framed art and
ephemera, their best vintage clothing, and delicate glassware and china that is
too good to risk at an outdoor market. The jewelry is impressive, too.

✠ where to park

On-site parking is available.

⚓ where to stay

Penn's View Hotel • see page 64

⚓ where to eat

There is plenty to munch at the market, or walk across the street to Philadelphia's only Venezuelan restaurant:

Sazon

941 Spring Garden Street • (215) 763-2500 • sazonphilly.com
Tuesday and Wednesday 5:30 pm to 9 pm; Thursday 5:30 pm to 10 pm;
Friday 5:30 pm to 11 pm; Saturday 11 am to 11 pm; Sunday 11 am to 9pm

The chef/owners are wizards with arepas and pure, South American chocolate. Venezuelan cuisine is largely gluten free, and there are many options for vegetarians and vegans. International and traditional brunch is served on Saturday and Sunday. BYOB; cash only.

⚓ nearby attractions

Edgar Allan Poe National Historic Site

532 North 7th Street • (215) 597-8780 • nps.gov/edal
Tours Wednesday through Sunday 9 am to 5 pm

A statue of a raven casts its shadow on this small brick house where Poe lived from 1843 to 1844 and may have written "Eulalie." The museum is reputed to be deliciously creepy.

What I bought: two charm bracelets, one with a tiny shoe and the other with a small Madonna, $10 for both.

What I passed up: 1870s earthenware whiskey bottle with the original label, $10.

What I will regret forever: pair of homemade sawhorses, $45.

Hardy Middle School Parking Lot
Wisconsin Avenue at 34th Street, NW
Washington, D.C.
Year round
Sunday, 8 am to 4 pm
georgetownfleamarket.com

georgetown flea market
washington, d.c.

Even though the Georgetown Flea opens at 8 am, there's something about it that invites a relaxed, slide-in-late kind of arrival, perfectly fitting with Sunday mornings in Georgetown. Slow, brunchy, no-make-up kinds of mornings. Maybe it's because it's been there every Sunday for 40 years, or the quiet setting, or the politicians in running shorts. Even the weather doesn't really matter unless it's raining hard or there's a blizzard. In that case the management recommends going to a movie instead.

The size is quite manageable. There are usually about a hundred vendors; most are selling antiques and vintage, with a few artisans who make jewelry, hats, and other fine items of desire. The people-watching is four-star. Someone once said this is the only place in the world where you might see a senator and a Supreme Court justice haggling over an armoire.

Then there's the literary connection. The market provided background for Larry McMurtry's novel *Cadillac Jack* (1984). McMurtry, who wrote *The Last*

Picture Show and won a Pulitzer Prize for *Lonesome Dove,* is a used book dealer, and had a shop called Booked Up on nearby 31st Street for over 30 years. His story of the antique dealer/rodeo cowboy Cadillac Jack is a rare portrait of the golden days of flea markets and auctions seen through the eyes of an itinerant dealer.

Pickings in this neighborhood have a certain character that conjures up images of pedigreed mansions, grande dames in sitting rooms, glittery cocktail parties, midnight intrigues, and quick exits. These things probably did not pass through the hands of Sister Parish and Albert Hadley, but you never know and it's fun to imagine.

In the category of antique or close to it, the market is strong in oil portraits, flatware (both sterling and plate), candlesticks, needlepoint, punchbowls, statuettes, alabaster lamps, clocks, and monogrammed tableware. There's a bit of furniture, mostly large, and lots of sweet Victorian smalls.

Mid-century modern furniture is another strength with accessories like lava-glazed lamps, small crystal chandeliers, art, and vintage linens all easy to find. Of the same period, watch for collectibles related to the nation's capital like campaign items, books, souvenirs of monuments and museums, and ephemera. On a more utilitarian level, there's a guy with a big selection of bicycles.

Another category here that may be unique to D.C. is international goods. At certain tables one could imagine that the dealer has just returned from yard sales on Embassy Row. There is much from Asia: kimonos, oil-paper umbrellas, carved chests, folding screens, painted porcelain, prints, books, and textiles. We also saw Cuban movie posters and African art.

✠ pets, etc.

According to the promoter, pets are allowed as long as they spend some money.

✠ getting there

The Flea is on the highest point in Georgetown, on Wisconsin Avenue at the intersection of 34th Street across from the so-called "Social" Safeway. The Georgetown-Union Station Circulator Bus stops right in front, operates every 10 minutes between 7 am and 9 pm, and costs only $1. The ride from Union Station takes about 45 minutes.

This itinerary is easy to navigate and everything is within a few blocks (see lodging, restaurants, and attractions below). The Holiday Inn is across the street from the market. Café Divan is half a block south of the market on the same side of the street and Bistrot Lepic is a few doors down from there. To reach the entrance to Dumbarton Oaks, take S Street east one block to 32nd Street and go one half block south.

✠ where to park

On-street parking is free on Sundays but might take some looking. For hints see georgetowndc.com.

✠ where to stay

Holiday Inn Georgetown
2101 Wisconsin Avenue, NW • (202) 338-4600 • holidayinn.com
Daily charge for parking. Free shuttle within 1.5-mile radius.

⚲ where to eat

Bistrot Lepic & Wine Bar

1736 Wisconsin Avenue, NW · (202) 333-0111 · bistrotlepic.com
Brunch: Saturday and Sunday 11 am to 3 pm; Lunch: Monday to Friday
11:30 am to 2:30 pm; Dinner: Sunday and Monday 5:30 pm to 9:30 pm;
Tuesday to Thursday 5:30 pm to 10 pm; Friday and Saturday 5:30 pm to
10:30 pm; Wine Bar: Daily 5:30 pm to midnight

Cozy dining downstairs, bar and couches upstairs. Live jazz one or two times a week.

Café Divan

1834 Wisconsin Avenue, NW · (202) 338-1747 · cafedivan.com
Monday to Friday 11 am to 10 pm; Saturday and Sunday 9 am to 11 pm;
Sunday 9 am to 11 pm; Brunch: Saturday and Sunday 9 am to 2 pm.

Modern Turkish cuisine in a shiny new glass-enclosed space.

⚲ nearby attractions

Dumbarton Oaks Research Library and Collection

Museum and museum shop entrance: 1703 32nd Street, NW (between
S and R Streets) · Garden entrance: 31st Street, NW (at R Street) · doaks.org
Museum and gardens: Tuesday to Sunday. In warm months, 2 pm to 6 pm;
in late fall and winter, 2 pm to 5 pm; closed Monday · No parking on grounds.

Shopping the Flea offers an excuse (if you need one) to see Dumbarton Oaks,
an early 19th-century estate that became the country house of Mildred Barnes
Bliss and Robert Woods Bliss and is now a legendary research center for Byzantine and Pre-Columbian studies and garden design. It's only a couple of

blocks away on the east side of Wisconsin Avenue. Visitors can tour the museums and collections of Byzantine and European art. Philip Johnson designed the modernist glass building that houses the Pre-Columbian collection. The gardens were designed by Beatrix Farrand, niece of Edith Wharton, who installed terraces and garden rooms in the manner of the Italian Renaissance. They are considered some of the finest in America, and are especially beautiful when the cherry trees are blooming.

What I bought: 1860s photograph of a young woman in a plaid bonnet, $12.

What I passed up: Set of Dionne quintuplet dolls in blue diapers, price unknown.

What I will regret forever: Bench with red velvet button-tufted upholstery and curved metal legs, price unknown.

US Route 40 from
Baltimore, Maryland to St. Louis, Missouri
First Wednesday through Sunday
following Memorial Day
Friday and Saturday have the most sales
Dawn to dusk (more or less)

the historic national road yard sale
maryland to missouri

There is no better excuse for a road trip than this 824-mile yard sale along America's oldest highway. Held every year just after Memorial Day weekend, it follows Historic National Road (US Route 40) out of Baltimore, crosses the Appalachian Mountains, dips into West Virginia and Pennsylvania, then rolls through the heartlands all the way to East St. Louis. Anything goes as lone farmers to entire towns drag their cast-offs to the road and the bargaining begins. It's a free-for-all of rubbernecking, brake-slamming shopping with gorgeous scenery and plenty of regional food. In a word: fabulous.

Thomas Jefferson, taking a hint from George Washington, began building the road in 1806. The objective was to connect the east with the fertile Ohio Valley. It originally began in Cumberland, Maryland, site of Washington's first military headquarters, and ended in Vandalia, Illinois, where Abraham Lincoln began his life in politics. Each mile was marked by a stone pillar giving the distance to the nearest towns. Some of these mile markers survive, particularly

in eastern Ohio near Zanesville where the National Road/Zane Grey Museum is located.

By 1830, 90,000 people a year were traveling the National Road. The road surface was so good that stagecoaches could travel seven miles an hour in dry weather as long as they avoided the families in wobbly wagons pulled by farm animals, and the herds of hogs, sheep, and turkeys that kept the travelers fed. Taverns proliferated, say, one every mile. Quoting *Harper's Magazine*, "never before were there such landlords, such taverns, such dinners, such whiskey. . . or such an endless cavalcade of coaches and wagons." Historic inns and sites still line the road; many are on the National Register of Historic Places.

The yard sale was founded by Patricia McDaniel, owner of Old Storefront

Antiques on the National Road in Dublin, Indiana. "We started planning for the road's bicentennial in 2006, and I wanted to bring people out to see the road with something everybody could afford to do, no matter their income. At yard sales you can always have a good time whether you're rich or just a kid with a dollar." She remains a devoted promoter and has published three editions of the *Historic National Road Yard Sale Cookbook*, filled with favorite recipes of sale participants.

Each year more sales pop up. They are particularly plentiful in Maryland, Ohio, and Indiana. The Historic National Road Yard Sale page on Facebook has running commentary on what's happening where. In Eastern Ohio, Licking County is a sure bet, with Muskingum County quickly catching up. "Antique

Alley" through Wayne County, Indiana, seems to have a sale at every third house on both sides of the street in Centerville and Cambridge City (both National Historic Districts) and countless barn sales in rural areas. Random sales open on Wednesday and Thursday; the best days are Friday and Saturday; Sunday is spotty.

It's not just homeowners who bring out their goods. Antique malls and shops keep longer hours during the sale, and pop-up stores appear in abandoned gas stations and old sheds. Clumps of parked cars ahead herald sales with the best stuff. Traffic can be heavy with gawking adding to the hazard factor, so extra caution for both drivers and pedestrians is a must.

✠ pets
Conditions will vary, use your best judgment on whether to take the dog along.

✠ getting there
Jump in the car and start at either end, or anywhere in the middle.

✠ where to park
Just stop the car along the road and get out.

✠ where to stay
There are historic inns, bed & breakfasts, and vintage motels along the road but don't expect vacancies. Booking well in advance is the best way to snag a room with a four-poster bed or a lava lamp. Here are a few suggestions (traveling east to west).

If you can't find a historic rest stop, Interstate 70, with the usual restaurant and hotel chains, parallels the National Road and is separated by only a mile or two at many points.

MARYLAND

Little Orleans Lodge Bed & Breakfast
12814 Appel Road, Little Orleans • (301) 478-210 • littleorleanslodge.net

Originally a one-room school, the building has been converted into rustic lodgings most appreciated by hikers, bikers, and outdoorsy folks. Baths are shared. The management advises that "children find our lodge very boring." Perhaps lingering schoolroom tedium is the culprit.

Town Hill Hotel Bed & Breakfast

31101 National Pike, Little Orleans • (301) 478-2794 • townhillbnb.com

Built in the 1920s, this was the "first tourist hotel built in the state of Maryland to accommodate the automobile traveler." It has 21 rooms and boasts views of three states.

PENNSYLVANIA

Century Inn 1794

2175 National Road East, Scenery Hill (one hour south of Pittsburgh)
(724) 945-6600 • centuryinn.com
Lunch: Wednesday though Sunday 11:30 am to 3 pm (reservations recommended);
Dinner: Sunday to Thursday 5 pm to 8 pm; Friday and Saturday 5 pm to 9 pm.

Open since 1794, this is the oldest continuously operating inn on the National Road. There are nine guest rooms and five historic dining rooms. Andrew Jackson, the Marquis de Lafayette, Henry Clay, General Santa Ana, and James K. Polk have all slept here. Thomas Jefferson's own recipe for creamy peanut soup is on the menu. Three additional rooms are available across the road at Zephanie Riggle's House of Entertainment.

WEST VIRGINIA

Lawrencefield Bed & Breakfast

360 Table Rock Lane, Wheeling • (304) 905-9991 • thelawrencefieldbandb.com

Rooms are furnished with antiques at this gracious 1845 brick mansion on landscaped grounds near Oglebay Park in Wheeling.

OHIO

Hillside Motel

54481 National Road, Bridgeport • (740) 635-9111 • hillside-motel.com

Vintage fans will appreciate this well-preserved example of a 1950s motel. Cabins and campgrounds are also available. Pets are welcome.

Baker's Motel

8855 East Pike, Norwich • (740) 872-3232 • bakersmotel.com

Family-owned for over 30 years, this vintage motel is across the road from the National Road/Zane Grey Museum and next door to an antique mall.

The Historic Buena Vista Motel

8518 East National Road, South Vienna • (937) 568-4904 historicbuenavistamotel.com

The first building on these grounds was a tavern built in 1826. In the 1930s, seven motor court cabins were added. The tavern survives as a private residence; three cabins remain of which at least one has been restored for overnight lodging.

Crawford's Market & Campgrounds

7968 East National Road, South Charleston • (937) 568-4266 ohiocamper.com/crawfordsmarket.html

The Crawfords are Yard Sale supporters and offer 300 RV sites plus tent-camping.

INDIANA

Philip W. Smith and Martha E. Parry Bed & Breakfast

2039 and 2221 E. Main Street, Richmond • (800) 966-8972 • pwsmithbnb.com

One Victorian and one Colonial Revival-style house comprise this B&B. Both houses are sumptuously furnished with antiques.

Historic Lantz House Inn
214 Old National Road, Centerville • (765) 855-2936 • lantzhouseinn.com

This small 1823 historic inn has an intimate garden with examples of Centerville's famous brick arches.

⚑ where to eat
It's best to catch lunch when you can. Small towns often have a diner, but many stop serving around 2 pm. Churches and schools set up food tents, and families grill burgers and hot dogs in their yards. It's possible to find barbequed chicken or a pork chop at a firehouse, farm, or community center.

⚑ information and museums

National Road/Zane Grey Museum
8850 East Pike (Route 40), Norwich, Ohio • (740) 872-3143
consumer.discoverohio.com
Wednesday to Friday 10 am to 4 pm; Saturday and Sunday 1 pm to 4 pm

This museum has a 136-foot diorama of National Road, plus exhibits on author Zane Grey, and an impressive collection of Ohio pottery.

The Old National Road Welcome Center
5701 National Road East, Richmond, Indiana • (800) 828-8414 • visitrichmond.org
Monday to Friday 8:30 am to 5 pm; Saturday 9 am to 5 pm; Sunday 9 am to 4 pm.
Closed on Sundays from November through April

Plentiful brochures, knowledgeable staff, and nice restrooms. Brochures and maps are available 24 hours a day in the foyer.

Historic National Road Yard Sale • facebook.com

For copies of the *Historic National Road Yard Sale Cookbook* e-mail Patricia McDaniel, info@oldstorefrontantiques.com.

National Road Yard Sale • facebook.com
This site is devoted to the sale in Licking County, Ohio.

Frank Brusca's Route 40 • Route40.net

Maryland Historic National Road • marylandnationalroad.org

National Road Heritage Corridor, Pennsylvania • nationalroadpa.org

Ohio National Road Association • ohionationalroad.org

Indiana's Historic National Road • indiananationalroad.org

National Road Association of Illinois • nationalroad.org

Porch Sitting Union of America • facebook.com

What I bought: oil painting of an Illinois banker, $12.50.

What I passed up: pair of lime-green, mid-century lamps, $30.

What I will regret forever: big box of ceramic figurines, $1.

Historic North Carolina State Fairgrounds
1025 Blue Ridge Road
Raleigh, North Carolina
Year round (except October)
Saturday and Sunday, 9 am to 6 pm
raleighfleamarket.net

raleigh flea market
raleigh, north carolina

Every Saturday morning except in October a lightning bolt crashes into the North Carolina State Fairgrounds, and when the smoke clears about half the 20th century has been brought back and is ripe for the picking. In October a different lightning bolt strikes and leaves behind the State Fair.

It's all about the vendors here; they're sharp as pimento cheese and friendly as whipped cream on a piece of pecan pie. Every single week they manage to get hold of wondrous things to make shoppers swoon, and they have plenty of tales to tell about what's what and where it came from. Those who pay attention can get an education along with their finds.

The flea market is in the southeast section of the Fairgrounds. Antiques and collectibles are outdoors, along with general merchandise and a yard sale section. There are more antiques and vintage inside two large exhibition halls. Hustle-bustle and higgledy-piggledy are fit descriptions—lots of people running around looking at piles of things and bargaining as fast as they can, while more people keep arriving.

Outside vendors include a couple with deep knowledge of vintage North Carolina pottery. Examples on their table included a batter bowl from J.B. Cole in Seagrove, some pieces by Virginia Shelton, a legendary potter who was known to throw standing up and barefoot, and a pottery reamer the likes of which I'd never seen. I learned about groundhog kilns, long horizontal kilns dug into the side of a hill that were peculiar to North Carolina in the 19th and early 20th centuries. I bought the reamer but when they heard I was taking it to the North, I had to promise to keep it warm.

Artist Mikel Robinson and his wife Kristina delight in photographic images. When they're not on the road showing his art, they're here selling antique photographs all the way back to daguerreotypes, ambrotypes, and tintypes, plus stacks of *cartes de visite* and cabinet cards. A box of X-rays was fascinating; another box had hundreds of black-and-white snapshots for $1 each. For the distance-challenged their Etsy store is Ephemera & Object, EandO.etsy.com.

Over on the far side near the road, those long rows of chairs belong to Chris McGinnis, aka "The Chairman." He earned his nickname selling chairs of all styles and periods, but also knows his antiques and often has very good Empire and Victorian pieces. There's a rumor that a certain show on the History Channel about picking antiques is going to shoot in Russia, and that The Chairman is involved.

Jacky Devaux started selling outdoors 13 years ago but now has a booth inside the Commercial Building. She specializes in English and European antiques. Her daughter lives in England and she visits her twice a year, bringing back

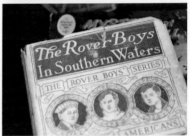

whatever she can. There are a couple of other vendors who carry similar stock. Any one of them would be happy to chat about (and correctly pronounce) faïence, Sèvres, Limoges, Staffordshire, Crown Devon, Meissen, etc. etc.

Molly Walker's booth in the same building is all vintage pink and blue kitchenware and china chickadees. She buys most of her merchandise in Pennsylvania where she's known as "Molly from Raleigh." When I found her she was laughing through her zebra-striped spectacles and giving short lessons on the history of sour cream glasses, prettily decorated glass jars that sour cream came in, often from Penn Maid Dairies in Philadelphia. The plastic lids are scarce.

The gold standard of weirdness is maintained at The Little Leviathan, also in the Commercial Building. Rod Sterling, who may or may not be connected to Miskatonic University in Arkham, Massachusetts, as his business card suggests, has assembled a museum/shop of delightfully dark objects right off the tip of imagination: conjoined skulls, surgical instruments, archaic books, absinthe bottles, scorpions on pins. The death's-head hawkmoths are my favorite.

⚘ pets, etc.
Pets are allowed but must be on leashes.

⚘ getting there
Raleigh, Durham, and Chapel Hill make up the Research Triangle, or just The Triangle. That title came about in the late 1950s when Research Triangle Park was founded in the center of a triangle formed by the three cities. It is the largest research park in the world, encompassing three universities and more than 150 companies from IBM to Burt's Bees. The local culture revolves

around it and the income it brings into the area. Raleigh-Durham Airport (RDU) is midway between Raleigh and the Research Park, and about 10 miles from the fairgrounds.

Enter the market at State Fairgrounds Gate 11 on Blue Ridge Road near Hillsborough Street. The market website has detailed directions.

⚓ where to park

There is free parking at the Fairgrounds.

⚓ where to stay

Every hotel chain is represented in the area; if you have a favorite brand there is probably a choice near your destination. See visitraleigh.com. B&B lovers should also check Durham, innsofdurham.com.

⚓ where to eat

At the market, lots of choices are offered from homemade cookies, doughnuts, and empanadas to the usual hot dogs, popcorn, and cotton candy. There are several food trucks. Inside the Commercial building, Carolina Treat Center has breakfast, sandwiches, ice cream, coffee, hot chocolate, and lemonade. More fair food is at the 1853 Grill, in the row of small shops near the arena.

Raleigh and surrounding towns have a huge culinary scene. *Southern Living* magazine named it one of the "Top 10 Tastiest Towns in the South." In addition, the Triangle was named one of America's top ten beer cities. There are far too many choices to name. See visitraleigh.com or pick up a copy of *Visit Raleigh* at the airport or a hotel.

Historic sweet treat: Krispy Kreme is a homemade North Carolina business that got its start in Winston-Salem in 1937 and still prompts kids to cross their fingers that the Hot Now (fresh baked) sign will be on when Dad or Mom drives by.

Krispy Kreme Doughnuts
549 North Person Street, Raleigh • (919) 833-3682 • krispykreme.com
Daily 6 am to midnight; Hot Light hours: 6 am to 11 am, 6 pm to 11 pm

⚲ nearby attractions

Historic Oakwood

Oakwood Avenue • historicoakwood.org

No antique lover should miss this neighborhood of post-Civil War Victorian homes on the east side of downtown Raleigh. Visitors from other cities will be astonished by the number of 19th-century homes that remain intact where any other town, especially a state capitol, would have long ago erected office buildings and parking garages. Oakwood Avenue is central, but the district extends from East Franklin Street on the north to New Bern Avenue on the south, and from North Person Street to Watauga Street from east to west. Homes vary in style from Neoclassical to Italianate, Queen Anne to Craftsman, with architectural details custom-designed for southern living and comfort. Look for porches with haint blue ceilings, a folkloric color that is thought to deter flies, wasps, and evil spirits.

Historic Oakwood Cemetery

701 Oakwood Avenue, Raleigh • (919) 832-6077 • historicoakwoodcemetery.com
Daily 8 am to 6 pm; 8 am to 5 pm in winter

The eastern border of Historic Oakwood is formed by beautifully landscaped Oakwood Cemetery, the burial place of many prominent North Carolinians with impressive and artistic monuments. Just inside the entrance the Stars and Bars fly over the Confederate Cemetery, which contains the graves of 1,500 soldiers who died for the South, many when they were barely 20 years old. The saddest section contains rows of graves marked "CSA Unknown." On top of the hill the House of Memory commemorates North Carolinians who died in all the wars before and after. Maps are available at the office.

What I bought: two X-rays of abstracted bones, $10.

What I passed up: chair made out of a spinning wheel, $30.

What I will regret forever: Candlewick glass punch bowl and under tray, $150.

1321 Atlanta Highway
Cumming, Georgia
Third weekend of every month
Friday 9 am to 5 pm
Saturday 9 am to 6 pm
Sunday 10 am to 5 pm
lakewoodantiques.com

lakewood 400 antiques market cumming, georgia

Every third weekend of the month the land of Scarlett O'Hara hosts a major flea and antique market, and because this is the steamy South it's in a big air-conditioned building. It may look like an antique mall from the outside but no antique mall ever approached the level of style and imagination displayed here. Even Martha Stewart's team might be jealous.

The location is relatively new. For years the market occupied several Spanish Colonial-style exhibition halls at the old Lakewood Fairgrounds in south Atlanta. The fairgrounds, which opened in 1916, were a wonderland of amusements with multiple Ferris wheels and a wooden roller coaster called the Greyhound. In 1971 a section of the coaster was blown up for a scene in *Smokey & the Bandit 2*. The current tenant is a major film studio.

The market is now in Cumming, about 40 miles northeast of Atlanta, just off Highway 400, which is known fondly as the Georgia Autobahn because of unrepentant speeders. The 45,000-square-foot building is shaped like a four-fingered letter E toppled on its back, with one hall in each finger and the long side divided into four more halls. Each hall has its own personality. A café anchors the central area at the main entrance.

Hundreds sell here. Antique experts, long-time collectors, vintage mavens, clever artisans; booth after booth is filled with surprises. Dealers in halls A through E set up every month, those in F through H are permanently settled in beautifully designed and merchandised spaces. A contingent including the garden and yard art crowd sells outdoors. There is very little flotsam; even if an item is not antique, vintage, or remade, it's guaranteed to be interesting, like the flora at Trixie's Carnivorous Plants. Services are available, too, including appraisals, jewelry repair, framing, and furniture restoration.

Some permanent dealers have taken their vision to the max. The white clapboard building resembling a cottage on Nantucket is Grosgrain Annie's Heirloom Ribbon Emporium. Jo Anne Rogers, mistress of trimmings, has filled it with spools and spools of vintage and antique ribbon, rickrack, and lace. Gesturing with her multicolored hands, she explains that her love in life is dyeing, anything from antique silk ribbon to cardboard string tags: "I'd dye my husband if he'd stand for it."

The secure, indoor nature of the market enables dealers to show rare and unusual items. As expected in the South, Confederate regalia, flags, and bits of Civil War uniforms are in evidence. At last visit there were stacks of Persian carpets, folios of botanical specimens, an eight-foot metal T-Rex, and a set of matching barber chairs.

The best overall design award might go to Hall H, with its vintage floral carpet

Vintage metal numbers &
Letters $1.00~15 for $10.00

and quirky booths. The first space is a candyland of stained glass windows, chandeliers, and lamps. The booth across the aisle is packed with vintage clothing. Down the way at So Then So Now, Sabrina Orangio's 20th-century curiosities are blithely displayed beneath signs hand-lettered on paper plates. Her booth is styled with a master's eye for fun; she hangs clothes from bright red faucets and uses clipboards to display shoes. Her neighbor across the aisle sports an edgy beach theme.

Much of the handmade jewelry and clothing is in Hall E. Sometimes artisans whose jewelry is carried by fancy stores set up here, offering seconds and discontinued lines at wholesale prices. There was a crowd around Cat's Carpetbags where Cat Goodrum's funky handmade backpacks and cell phone bags were selling like crazy. With a sharp eye to the past, she sews everything herself on an antique sewing machine and is on a campaign to bring back bloomers.

Many of the finds in Hall F can be labeled guy stuff. The entrance is marked by rows of antique gas pumps and service station signs. This leads into a tunnel of massive wooden cabinets from forgotten stores and public institutions, some still containing remnants of cloudy medicine bottles or a stray drum major's hat.

All in all, there's a lot of stuff here—a huge amount, actually—from crates of doorknobs to those gas pumps and that T-Rex. There should also be motorcycles and cars with fins, and a tightrope walker with a long pole overhead. You can take the flea out of the fairgrounds but you'll never get the fairgrounds out of this flea.

⚑ getting there

From Highway 400 take exit 13, turn right on Highway 9 (Atlanta Highway) and go 1.5 miles. There is only one entrance, watch for the "Antiques!" signs along the road. The small ($3 in 2013) admission fee is good for all three days.

⚑ where to park

There is plenty of free parking on the side and in back of the building.

⚑ where to stay

Cumming is situated on the north side of Atlanta at the foot of the north Georgia mountains near Lake Sidney Lanier. Depending on mood, a weekend visit to the flea market can be either an urban jaunt or a country getaway.

Hilton Garden Inn North Atlanta/Alpharetta

4025 Windward Plaza Drive, Alpharetta, Georgia • (770) 360-7766

hiltongardeninn3.hilton.com

This is the official hotel of the market just under ten miles away, in a tranquil setting not far from North Point Mall. It offers special rates to flea market attendees. Book early; ask for Lakewood 400 group rate.

Most national chains have a hotel in the Cumming/Alpharetta area.
See cummingforsythchamber.org and awesomealpharetta.com for locations.

Both resorts below are located in scenic areas and have amenities including golf courses. They are ideal for shoppers with spouses who are not junkers and who prefer other amusements.

Chateau Élan Inn, Winery, and Spa

100 Rue Charlemagne, Braselton • (800) 233-WINE • chateauelan.com

Guests here can play golf, visit the spa, go hiking or horseback riding, and enjoy fine dining and wine tastings.

Lake Lanier Islands Resort

7000 Lanier Islands Parkway, Buford • (770) 945-8787 • lakelanierislands.com

A resort offering dining, a spa, golf, tennis, hiking, boating, and zip lines.

⚓ where to eat

The café at the market serves just about everything found on the menu at a typical state fair; the market is somewhat isolated, so it make sense to eat here.

Sal's Place

111 West Courthouse Square, Cumming • (770) 887-3730 • sals-place.com
Tuesday to Friday 11 am to 9 pm; Saturday 4 pm to 11 pm;
closed Sunday and Monday

Locals love the pizza here.

Tam's Backstage

215 Ingram Avenue, Cumming • (678) 455-8310 • tamsbackstage.com
Lunch: Monday to Friday 11 am to 4 pm; Dinner: Monday to Thursday 4 pm
to 9:30 pm; Friday and Saturday 4 pm to 10 pm; closed Sunday.

Chef/owner Kelly Tam serves American cuisine with an Italian flair in an
historic 1927 schoolhouse. Reservations are recommended.

Tara Humata Mexican Grill & Tequila Bar

6195 Windward Parkway, Alpharetta • (770) 772-4540 • tarahumata.com
Monday to Thursday 11 am to 10:30 pm; Friday and Saturday 11 am to
midnight; Sunday 11 am to 10 pm

You'll find this south of the border café, with patio and 150 kinds of tequila,
just around the corner from the Hilton.

Sushi Nami Japanese Restaurant

5316 Windward Parkway, Alpharetta • (678) 566-3889 • sushinami.com
Lunch: Monday to Friday 11:30 am to 2:30 pm; Dinner: Sunday to Thursday
5 pm to 10 pm; Friday and Saturday 5 pm to 11 pm

Fresh, imaginative sushi is served in this hip restaurant near the Hilton.

✝ nearby attractions

Alpharetta's home design center: Two huge antique and home design stores on North Main Street

Queen of Hearts Antiques and Interiors

670 North Main Street (Alpharetta Highway) • (678) 297-7571

queenofheartsantiques-interiors.com

Monday to Saturday 10 am to 6 pm, Thursdays until 8 pm; Sunday noon to 6 pm

Continue shopping for antiques and home décor at this 30,000-square-foot antique mall.

Home Fashion Interiors

793 North Main Street • (770) 664-9544 • homefashioncenter.com

Monday to Saturday 10 am to 7 pm; Sunday noon to 5 pm

People are always talking about the trick of combining antiques and vintage findings with new furniture. Browse this 27,000-square-foot locally-owned furniture showroom for ideas. Located across the road from Queen of Hearts.

What I bought: Iroquois war club, $75.

What I passed up: Civil War-era shoo-fly fan, $100.

What I will regret forever: oil copy of Vermeer's painting *A Girl Reading a Letter by an Open Window*, $850.

20651 New U.S. Highway 441
just north of Rt. 46
(352) 383-8593

antique extravaganza
Third weekend in November,
January, and February
Friday 10 am
Saturday and Sunday 8 am

antique fair
March through October and December
Third weekend of the month
Saturday and Sunday 9 am to 5 pm

antique center
Year round
Friday 10 am to 4 pm
Saturday and Sunday 9 am to 5 pm

street of shops
Year round
Saturday and Sunday 9 am to 5 pm

farmers market & flea market
Year round
Saturday and Sunday 8 am to 4 pm

renningers.com

renninger's antique center and farmers & flea market
mt. dora, florida

Ah, Mt. Dora. This market has something for everyone even if they have no interest in antiques and are just after fresh vegetables for soup. Thirty minutes north of Orlando in the Harris Chain of Lakes country, the town can stand alone as a place to visit/shop/eat, but add this huge market and it gets the Fab Place To Live/ Love/Retire Award. It might thrive because dealers with umpteen years of experience had the same thought and, dreaming of warm breezes, hauled their remaining treasures down I-95 to the very center of Florida where they decamped for good.

Renninger's operates two markets in Pennsylvania, in Kutztown and Adamstown, and this one in Florida. All are based on the same formula in hopes of pleasing everyone. Take a big piece of land and set up a weekend flea market of the old mold with household needs, car parts, jars of jam, produce, general junk, and the dreaded tube socks. Then add an Antique Center, a pleasant air-conditioned building with permanent booths for superior dealers that is also open every weekend. Throw in monthly antique fairs that bring in 300 more dealers, and several annual extravaganzas that draw 800 dealers and the shoppers start arriving.

Mt. Dora's three Extravaganza weekends are in the winter when the weather is at its best. It's a thrill to be outside in January and see all the antiques lined up in the shade of live oaks trimmed in Spanish moss. The pickings are endless, from pedigreed colonial through graceful mid-century modern to funky late 20th century. Furniture, toys, linens, quilts, doors and windows, things forgotten and now remembered. It's a good thing the sale is three days long; one could easily wander from morning until dusk and cover only a portion of the market. There's a lot of walking, some in rough terrain, so do choose sneakers over flip-flops.

There's no need to wait for an Extravaganza to enjoy Florida's wealth of antiques. Renninger's Antique Center is open every week from Friday through Sunday. The wares in close to 200 booths show amazing diversity from all time periods and most continents. Friday is a quiet day; some booths are closed. Saturday and Sunday are busy with lots of shoppers. There is no central cashier. Pay the dealer directly; if there is no one at the booth just ask one of the nearby dealers to make the sale. They are happy to do it.

A few highlights: At Booth D-18 not far from the café, David Law and Ed Attzenhoffer welcome browsers like old friends and show off their eclectic collection that shouldn't make sense but in their hands does. Silver snuff boxes

and celluloid shoehorns, rosaries and beaded fruit, Mt. Dora memorabilia and books, books, books, many quite rare. They have another booth across the aisle that's all vintage. Robert Cauthen, Booth F-22, has unusual articles related to photography, both still and motion picture: antique cameras, magazines, darkroom items, and projectors. Near the main entrance at Booth G-2, Francis and Lynelle Lynch have fine estate jewelry, and new pieces reconstructed from reclaimed gold and jewels. Mr. Lynch says that gold has been recycled for centuries, and that any piece of antique jewelry could very well contain gold from the sack of Rome. Wouldn't that be a find?

A nice twist to Mt. Dora is the Street of Shops. It isn't a cute a Disneyesque reproduction; it's a real alleyway of southern vernacular cottages made of tin and boards and spit, each tailored to the vision of its owner and filled with wonderful rare bits of American stuff.

The cabin with the lightning bolt Zenith sign belongs to Ted Miguel who repairs and sells vintage electronics. In the dim interior, flickering oscilloscopes, VU meters, and tube testers induce flashbacks of 1950s sci-fi. Radios, reel-to-reel tape players, turntables, and televisions with picture tubes fill all available corners. There is even a stocky Dumont TV like the one we had when I was a little girl and crazy about Princess Summerfall Winterspring from the Howdy-Doody Show.

The sign outside the building that appears to house a curated yard sale advertises "Tons of Stuff and Cold Air." Inside is a perfectly catalogued hoarder's library of mid-century minutiae. Tiny ceramic elephants and heavy restaurant coffee cups call to me. In order to keep the stacks full the owner says she faithfully shops estate sales, yard sales, and a flea market and rescues an average of three boxes of vintage trinkets every week.

The corner is anchored by Better With Age Antique Interiors, situated in two connecting buildings. In one, proper English antiques and lodge gear meet Hemingway in Key West, meaning ships and saddles and pipes. The other side has things for the garden. All around, decaying furniture and statuary are slowly and picturesquely being absorbed by Florida's lush vegetation. Aesthetics here are first rate.

Try to schedule some time in Mt. Dora, a shady lakeside town with crackerjack architecture where Presidents Calvin Coolidge and Dwight Eisenhower once had winter retreats. It's a walker's town filled with antiques, shops, restaurants, inns, and B&Bs. For the foot-worn there with many sidewalk cafes, some over-looking the water.

⚱ getting there
The market is a 40-minute drive north of the Orlando airport, just east of the town of Mt. Dora. There are no interstates nearby; follow Route 441, a four-lane divided highway. Free maps of Florida are available at the airport's central information booth.

⚱ where to park
There are acres of free parking on the market grounds.

⚱ where to stay
Downtown Mt. Dora has 15 inns and B&Bs. There are a few chain hotels on Route 441. For complete listings see mountdora.com. Book well ahead for Extravaganza weekends.

Lakeside Inn

100 N. Alexander Street, Mt. Dora • (800) 556-5016 • lakeside-inn.com

The Lakeside Inn in downtown Mt. Dora is Florida's oldest continually operating hotel and the largest in town. Open since 1883, this 87-room historic hotel has long porches, rocking chairs, and water views.

⚑ where to eat

The Grub Hub Café

Inside the Antique Center on Aisle D, follow signs to "Restaurant"
Friday 9 am to 3:30 pm; Saturday and Sunday 9 am to 4:30 pm

The food here is so good the cafe has become a destination. Chef/owner Mandy Cushman cooks everything to order. Breakfast is served until 11 am. The cheeseburger trumps many a gourmet restaurant and the tarragon chicken salad can't be beat. Desserts are homemade too. There's a cute dining area where vintage kitchen tables bask under murals of the Dora Canal.

There are at least 20 restaurants in downtown Mt. Dora. Among the choices are a romantic bistro, a Cuban restaurant, and seafood with a view.

The Goblin Market Restaurant

330 Dora Drawdy Way • (352) 735-0059 • thegoblinmarketrestaurant.com
Lunch: Tuesday to Saturday 11 am to 3 pm; Sunday 11:30 to 3:30; Dinner: Tuesday to Thursday 5 pm to 9 pm; Friday and Saturday 5 pm to 10 pm; lounge open all day

This is a local favorite, with a cozy library-like atmosphere. Reservations are a must.

Copacabana Cuban Café

320 Dora Drawdy Way • (352) 385-9000 • copacabanacubancafe.com

Monday to Thursday, Sunday 11 am to 9 pm; Friday, Saturday 10am to 10 pm.

Imaginative Cuban food and prizewinning mojitos are served inside or on the large, covered patio.

Pisces Rising

239 West Fourth Avenue • (352) 385-2669 • www.piscesrisingdining.com

Monday to Thursday, 11:30 am to 9 pm; Friday and Saturday 11:30 am to 10 pm; Sunday 11 am to 9 pm

Near Lake Dora with sunset views at cocktail hour, this restaurant specializes in fresh fish, seafood, and steaks.

⚓ nearby attractions

The Dora Canal

Near Wooten Park in Tavares

For guided boat tours see doracanaltour.com or call The Rusty Anchor (352) 383-3933.

The Dora Canal is a short waterway connecting Lake Dora and Lake Eustis. In the 1930s a sports writer called this "the most beautiful mile of water in the world." Beloved by birders and naturalists, it's known for ancient cypress trees, myriads of water birds, otters, turtles, and alligators. There is a persistent rumor that Hollywood came here to shoot retakes for *The African Queen*.

✈ seaplane rides

Jones Brothers & Company Air and Sea Adventures

150 East Ruby Street, Tavares • (352) 508-1800 • jonesairandsea.com.

To see the Chain of Lakes from the air, travel a few miles north on US 441 to Tavares, which calls itself "America's Seaplane City," a claim validated by areas marked "Seaplane Parking Only." The Jones Brothers, Henry and Walton, will be delighted to schedule a tour that leaves from Wooten Park, or pick up at a private location, a real treat for wedding or family reunions. Choose a tour route from their menu or design a custom route anywhere within a 25-mile radius.

What I bought: delicate gray handkerchief with red and black deco style monogram appliqued by hand, $1.

What I passed up: eighteen-inch metallic apple made by Disney's prop department, $69.

What I will regret forever: terrific copy of Guido Reni's portrait of Beatrice Cenci, my favorite Renaissance heroine, $675.

Lincoln Road Mall
(from Lenox Avenue through
Meridian Avenue)
Miami Beach, Florida
Mid-October to the first weekend in May
Every other Sunday, 8 am to 6 pm
antiquecollectiblemarket.com

lincoln road antique & collectible market
miami beach, florida

Boys and girls can play for hours at this winter market in, yes, glamorous Miami Beach, where the right sunglasses are as precious as a shoebox of diamonds. Scores of dealers set up along Lincoln Road in South Beach, squeezed in between sidewalk cafés. The hungry and hungover need not suffer; coffee or brunch can be had every nine paces, and an eye can be kept on that Hollywood Regency lamp while sipping a Bloody Mary. Sometimes it's hot or rainy, but who cares when there are finds like these to covet?

There are usually about 125 dealers; a surprising number are from New York City and New England. The majority of shoppers are Europeans, New Yorkers, and Floridians who live between Palm Beach and Key West. When a big event like Art Basel is in town, merchandise changes to suit the crowd. During that show in early December, art of all periods and styles shows up for sale at the market.

The scene is Lincoln Road Mall, which is not a stuffy indoor shopping center like up north, but rather an esplanade of fancy shops and restaurants with tropical flora down the middle. Thirty-foot palm trees are reminders that we are not in Ohio anymore. White pop-up tents extend for blocks, each shading a vendor and their beguiling collections.

Dealers swear that promoters Louis Bondi and Tony Angione have come up with the best show in America. It's been around for 20+ years and is based on big city antique markets like ones Biondi used to orchestrate in Berlin. The setting is prime; it's hard to top a sunny Sunday in an urban tropical paradise, with great pickings, great food, and great people watching. One jewelry dealer from New York says she does 50 shows a year and this is her favorite.

The proof, however, is in the browsing. The best things are nabbed early. Interior design professionals search for perfect accents for their latest clients; stylists are out for vintage designer clothing and accessories. They're there because they know it's possible to find pieces by top mid-century designers like George Nelson and Anne Fogarty.

Both designer and vintage clothing are easy to find. At Niki Simon Blacker's double booth near Lenox Avenue, a striking woman models an exquisite Thierry Mugler jacket and later a pair of fanciful sunglasses. Next door, men are ogling cufflinks at a booth that sells only cufflinks. Chanel bags, Versace bracelets—all are there for anyone with the patience to look. I found two Schiaparelli hats, each priced under $100.

Jewelry is everywhere: gold and silver, precious stones and paste, pearls and beads, Italian micro-mosaics and *pietra dura*, stacks and stacks of Bakelite and Lucite, and gallons of costume. One can spend as much or as little as one likes, but no one has to go home without a piece of jewelry.

The furniture here dates roughly from 1800 to 1980. There are plenty of selections for both classicists and modernists, but the emphasis is on post-World War II design because mid-century modern furniture is perfectly suited to one of Miami's signature architectural styles, MiMo (Miami Modern). Art Deco, for which Miami is famous, is also well represented and has many followers. Chairs, tables, and patio furniture are plentiful. There are piles of lamps, paintings, screens, pottery, vases, dishes, and swanky barware.

In the miscellaneous category, there are a couple of vinyl dealers who are sought after by DJs and the growing faction that believes LPs sound better than digital music. Typewriters from the 1960s and '70s are another anomaly that is popping up. These make excellent gifts for enigmatic students and can amuse small children for hours.

Now, on to borderline-tacky as only Miami Beach can do it. Seen: vintage poodle purses, various ashtrays sporting alligators, child's tricycle done up like a Harley, cigarette case with octopus decoration, many gold and crème telephones, Vikingesque helmet displayed atop a fire hydrant, lamp made of fish and seaweed set in Lucite, mosaic of fish, fish bottle opener, flower pot decorated with fish, enameled picture of fish. The winner? A gilded wheelchair upholstered with tiger skin faux-fur.

Later in the day the mall turns into a block party as neighbors with kids and dogs come out for brunch and an afternoon stroll. By 5 pm dealers are packing up and tents are coming down, but fun continues until the restaurants close at midnight or 1 am.

✠ pets, etc.

Pets are welcome.

✠ getting there

If going to the market from Miami, it's necessary to cross Biscayne Bay—but don't take one of those boring interstate bridges. The lovely Venetian Causeway (embarks at North West 15th Street) is a fantasy of white stucco bridges and blue water that travels across the Venetian Islands, six artificial islands built in the 1920s. Their names are, from west to east, Biscayne Island, San Marco Island, San Marino Island, Di Lido Island, and Rivo Alto Island.

When you reach Miami Beach, you're only a few blocks from the market. Follow 17th Street and take the first right on West Avenue where there are several parking lots, or continue on 17th and park in a garage (see Where to park).

Short of a salmon pink T-bird the hippest mode of transportation is a bicycle, preferably with a wire basket containing a chihuahua. It's easy to rent a bike but it could be difficult to borrow a dog.

DecoBike

Locations on Lincoln Road: Lincoln Road and West Avenue, Lincoln Road and Lenox Avenue (Pottery Barn), Lincoln Road and Jefferson Avenue, Lincoln Lane and Euclid Avenue • (305) 532-9494 • decobike.com • Seven days a week, 24 hours a day

DecoBike is a public bike sharing and rental program operated by the City of Miami Beach. There are over 100 locations to rent, switch, or return a bike. Download the free app or watch the video on the website to see how it works.

DESIGNER LABEL
&
NAME BRAND NECKTIES
2 FOR $20.
OR
$12. each

⚓ where to park

There's a parking garage north of Lincoln Road between Meridian and Pennsylvania Avenues. Surface lots on West Street and 17th Street have parking meters that are good for several hours but eat a lot of change. Best to pick up a roll of quarters.

⚓ where to stay

The hotels are near or on the ocean on the east coast of Miami Beach. Rooms start at $50 per night and can top $1,000: it depends on what you're looking for. Expect to pay for parking and possibly a deposit. Staying on the mainland is also an option. See mdpl.com for a list of hotels that support architectural preservation or tripadvisor.com.

⚑ where to eat

Pick any restaurant on Lincoln Road. Your feet may tell you when it's time to sit down. A couple of suggestions are:

Segafredo
1040 Lincoln Road near Lenox Avenue • (305) 673-0047 • sze-originale.com
Monday to Thursday, Sunday 10:30 am to 1 am; Friday and Saturday
10:30 am to 2 am

Sit on a velvet chair under the red umbrellas, sipping cappuccino and watching the bright, the beautiful, and the bizarre pass by.

Yardbird Southern Table & Bar

1600 Lenox Avenue • (305) 538-5220 • runchickenrun.com

Sunday 10 am to 11 pm; Monday to Thursday 11:30 am to 11 pm; Friday and Saturday 10 am to midnight

Chef Jeff McInnis serves chicken and waffles, biscuits, and grits for brunch, and fried chicken all the time.

⚓ nearby attractions

Art Deco District Walking Tours

Miami Design Preservation League and Art Deco Gift Shop

1001 Ocean Drive, Miami Beach • (305) 672-2014 • mdpl.org

Daily 9:30 am to 7 pm

Don't forget to look at the architecture. The Miami Design Preservation League leads prize-winning tours of iconic Miami design districts. Choose from the Official Art Deco Tour, MiMo (Miami Modern) Tour, Gay & Lesbian Walking Tour, Jewish Miami Beach Tour, Self-Guided Audio Tour, or various specialty tours. Tours take place daily and leave from the Art Deco Gift Shop.

What I bought: set of six mid-century cocktail glasses in rainbow colors, $25.

What I passed up: bright red surfboard, price unknown.

What I will regret forever: copy of *Cary Grant: The Lonely Heart* by the author of *The Duchess of Windsor: The Secret Life*, $8.

Clarke County Fairgrounds,
4401 S. Charleston Pike (Route 41)
Springfield, Ohio

extravaganza
Third weekend in May and September
Friday early bird admission 7 am to noon
regular admission noon to 6 pm
Saturday 8 am to 5 pm
Sunday 9 am to 4 pm

antique show and flea market
Third weekend in March, April, October,
and week of July 4th

springfieldantiqueshow.com

springfield antique show & flea market
springfield, ohio

Springfield is a town of 60,000 in southwest Ohio, with good reason to be visited. It was smart enough during the tear-'em-down '70s to hang on to its historic buildings and boasts old government and industrial edifices of height, charm, and mystery. It is the birthplace of the silent Lillian Gish, star of D.W. Griffith's masterpiece *Broken Blossoms*. It has an interesting Frank Lloyd Wright house. And it calls itself Antiquing Capital of the Midwest.

There are several antique markets at the county fairgrounds during the warm months, but the real event is the Springfield Extravaganza, one of the largest fleas in the Midwest. It is known for country antiques and primitives and is often featured in decorating magazines. Held twice a year in May and September, it has about 2,500 dealers; many have been coming for years. The market opens at 7 am on Friday and the rush begins. Only shoppers with desperately needy collections need endure this. The calm and rested shopper arrives two hours later after a nice breakfast.

The fairgrounds are on the southeast side of Springfield near Interstate 70. Those who prefer sightseeing to freeway driving can approach from the town side where yard sales are plentiful when the show is on. The double line of cars moving slowly toward the parking area is not inviting, so, if possible, opt for parking along the side of the road or in the grassy field to the right of the gate like the regulars do. If you do park outside the gate, look for the ticket seller as you walk in lest he chase you down.

At the main entrance the market seems small, nestled cozily under shade trees. Soon other rows of booths become visible, then more and more and the search is on. In no time at all you will be lost and very happy. The fairground is vast. Aisles of booths circle four exhibit buildings in the center of the grounds, which house quality antique dealers. There are more booths in the cattle, rabbit, sheep, and produce barns.

Some of the seasoned dealers with older and more valuable antiques begin to pack up around 3 pm on Friday and don't come back, so give your first attention to them. Younger hungry ones and those inside the four exhibit buildings stay for the whole weekend.

A highlight of this market is pottery and glassware made in Ohio by famous companies like Roseville, McCoy, Rookwood, Heisey, and Cambridge. From the mid-19th to mid-20th century, these and many other factories produced thousands of functional and decorative pieces for the home, from simple McCoy planters to elegant stemmed wine glasses. These collectibles are starting to become scarce but not here in Springfield where the best of the best still turns up and prices are low. Younger shoppers who are not familiar with etched stemware by Tiffin,

Cambridge, Fostoria, and others have an opportunity to discover beautiful mid-century wine and water glasses for prices below that of new ones sold in big box stores.

A new addition is Vintage Marketplace. Rather than cave to the tube-sock aesthetic as some markets have, Springfield's smart promoters persuaded the Etsy crowd to bring their refreshed, remade, and reloved merchandise to the fairgrounds and erected several large tents to house all of them in one place. The result is a fest of imagination and vintage style: pastel petticoats, classic wedding gowns, jeweled top hats, conglomerate jewelry, flowery lighting, urbane table settings, wearable religious artifacts, and lots of reinvented furniture. Even a bit of French country.

In the same vein, a team of young writers and photographers from Kentucky chose the extravaganza to launch their glossy new magazine, *Folk*. They filled the goat barn with junkers, artists, muskmelons, flags, canned tomatoes, red geraniums, and copies of the mag. Their editorial policy is devoted to slow life in the South, gardens, well-worn clothes, porch swings, heirloom food, sweet tea, and local everything. Things on everyone's wish list. See folklifestyle.com.

Those who accomplish a full circle of the grounds deserve a hand at the end of the day. For help transporting furniture and large items to the car, call (317) 431-7715 and give the number of the booth and approximate size of the piece.

If still in the mood for shopping, there are two huge antique malls a teacup's throw away. Springfield Antique Center is down the road from the fairgrounds on the other side of the interstate. Heart of Ohio, which has superb merchandise, is at Exit 62. The malls usually keep longer hours during the extravaganza, and are often open until 9 pm.

Heart of Ohio Antique Center
4785 East National Road (Rt. 40) at Exit 62 • (937) 324-2188
heartofohioantiques.biz • Daily 9:30 am to 6 pm

Springfield Antique Center
1735 Titus Road at Exit 59 • (937) 322-8868 • springfieldantiquecenter.webs.com
Daily 10 am to 6 pm

⚑ getting there
Springfield is midway between Columbus, Ohio, and the Indiana state line on
Route 40, Historic National Road. The market is south of town less than a mile
from Interstate 70, Exit 59.

⚲ where to stay

There are a dozen chain hotels along I-70 near the market.
See greaterspringfield.com.

Courtyard by Marriott Springfield Downtown

100 South Fountain Avenue, Springfield • (937) 322-3600 • marriott.com

The Marriott offers an antiquers special during the show with a reduced room rate including breakfast for two. It overlooks a six-story mural that salutes vaudeville impresario Gus Sun and hometown movie stars Lillian and Dorothy Gish. Book well in advance.

Houstonia Bed & Breakfast

25 East Mound Street, South Charleston • (937) 462-8855 • houstonia.net

This Prairie Victorian-Style house, formerly home of a famous Ohio robber baron, is ten minutes from the market.

Simon Kenton Inn

4690 Urbana Road, Springfield • (937) 399-9950 • simonkentoninn.com

Dinner: Tuesday to Saturday 5 pm to 11 pm; Sunday 11 am to 2 pm; closed Monday

An historic inn with fine dining and a pub, built on land owned by a frontiersman whose farm was the first white settlement in Ohio. The current Federal-style structure was built in 1828.

Victoria Green Plain Farm Bed and Breakfast

8606 Selma Pike, South Charleston • (937) 360-4082 • greenplain.com

This restored log cabin, built in 1815, sleeps six guests on three floors, and is surrounded by 65 acres and seven miles of nature trails.

⚑ where to eat

J & J's Cafe is located in the Mercantile Building at the fairgrounds; other food vendors are here and there. Crazy Uncle Larry's Pork Chop Roadhouse is in front of the Youth Building and his gourmet burgers are sold in the hub at the back of the exhibit buildings. Ice cream is found under the large inflated cone.

Cecil and Lime Café

227 East Cecil Street, Springfield • (937) 322-7950 • cecilandlime.com

Wednesday and Thursday 5 pm to 9 pm; Friday and Saturday 5 pm to 9:30 pm

This locally owned café with an American menu has a full bar and a patio.

✛ nearby attractions

The Westcott House

1340 East High Street, entrance at 85 South Greenmount Avenue, Springfield

westcotthouse.org

Museum and shop: Wednesday to Saturday 11 am to 5 pm; Sunday 1 pm to 5 pm

Guided tours only; reservations (937) 327-9291

Anyone interested in antiques or architecture should try to see this recently restored Frank Lloyd Wright house while visiting Springfield.

✛ websites

greaterspringfield.com

springfieldohioantiques.com

What I bought: framed diploma of Tupperware sales trainee signed by Tupperware goddess Brownie Wise, $10.

What I passed up: hand-painted cook stove from a 19th-century chuck wagon, $395.

What I will regret forever: little brooch with pearls, $15.

345 South Van Buren Street (State Route 5)
Shipshewana, Indiana

shipshewana antique market
Trading Place Pavilion,
368 South Van Buren Street
First Saturday in June, August, and
September, 7 am to 4 pm

flea market
May 1 to October 31
Every Tuesday and Wednesday
8 am to 5 pm

antique auction
Year round
Wednesday 9 am

livestock auction
Year round
Wednesday 11 am

horse auction
Year round
Friday 9 am

TradingPlaceAmerica.com

shipshewana auction & flea market
shipshewana, indiana

The last place you'd expect to find a 100-acre flea market with all the trimmings is the tiny town of Shipshewana in northeast Indiana, center of the second largest Amish community in the United States. Also called the Plain People, the Amish live a 19th-century lifestyle, dress in simple clothes, grow their hair and beards long, and travel via horse-drawn vehicles or bicycles. Their whitewashed homes and barns, perfectly manicured flower gardens, and endless pastures where goats and little lambs play tag make Shipshewana a lovely place to visit as well as a major tourist attraction.

Coming into town it's hard not to gape at all the buggies. The horses, proud country stock with their heads held high, clip-clop along in the slow lane like they own the road, ignoring the huffy-puffy lines of cars and RVs poking along toward the flea market.

Meet the Amish, who somehow manage to maintain their composure in spite of the 50,000 people who pass through every year.

To residents of the 21st century, the Amish are both picturesque and inscrutable. Members of a religious sect that descended from Swiss Anabaptists in the 16th century, they escaped persecution in Europe by coming to America under the wing of William Penn. They believe in being calm and humble, respecting nature, tilling the land, and raising large families.

The Amish don't believe in baptizing infants, only adults who have consciously decided to join the church. Children attend school through the eighth grade, then as teenagers go through a rite of passage called rumspringa, "a year off," to experience the modern world before committing to the sect. Some return to marry and start families, others leave the church. A former Amishman remembers that he only needed one ride on a Harley-Davidson to make up his mind.

The Shipshe (as locals call it) Flea is set up in the center of town on the east side of the road. Two big white auction buildings and a restaurant front the huge grounds. Admission is free. There's an information booth at the entrance with an attendant who hands out market guides and answers questions. It is well stocked with brochures for area lodging, restaurants, shopping, and nearby attractions.

It all began in 1922 when a man named George Curtis successfully auctioned six pigs, seven cows, and several head of young cattle at his farm, starting a business that evolved into the current auction and flea market. It differs from other markets in this book, having new merchandise along with antiques and a farmers market. With more than 600 dealers there is quite a range of merchandise. In an afternoon one can browse country kitchen collectibles, buy homemade candles, try on vintage hats, and stock up on school, craft, and office

supplies. One booth sells only varieties of scissors. Another is devoted to the needs of Red Hat Ladies. Antique sellers are mixed in, including a nice man whose specialty is vintage fishing equipment.

The farmers market is to the right of the entrance gate. Vendors are mainly Amish who bring fruits and vegetables, plants and flowers, jams and pickles. All are fresh off the farm. Sausage bread goes fast at the Bread Box Bakery booth. Those who crave protein can cross the parking lot to Yoder Meats & Cheese, a wonderland of cheese, sausage, jerky, and forgotten lunchmeat like headcheese and souse. Samples are offered but signs caution not to double-dip.

Plan to do the flea market on Tuesday and save Wednesday for the auction, which starts on the dot of 9 and continues until about 3. This is where the bulk of antiques are—furniture of all periods including mid-century modern, paintings, quilts, sets of china, farm tools, collectible toys, dolls—all sold in a cyclone of jump-and-shout with up to 12 auctioneers working simultaneously. Don't miss it. Those who've brought their trailer can nip next door to the livestock auction and pick up a cow or two.

If the market and auction don't satisfy the need for antiques, the Antique Gallery, with 31,000 square feet of browsing, is just across the road. It's open 9 am to 6 pm from May to September, and 10 am to 5 pm the rest of the year, every day except Sunday.

⚑ shopping

Note: The Amish don't allow photographs to be taken of themselves or their businesses, and prefer no one photographs or pets their horses. Buggies should be treated with courtesy. Pass when the traffic allows and never honk. Amish businesses accept cash and checks only and are closed all day on Sunday. Farms are private property but those advertising goods or services welcome visitors. The Amish do enjoy a good conversation if they are in the mood.

The Amish are superb craftsmen who make tables and chairs, desks, shelves, and bedroom sets from a myriad of woods including quarter-sawn oak.

Ervin's Millwork Shop
Booth 558-560 at the market or three miles south of town on Route 5 across from Meadowview School • (260) 768-7602 • Open market hours

Lambright Woodworking
7785 W 300 S., Topeka • (260) 593-2997
Monday to Friday 8 am to 4:30 pm; Saturday 9 am to 4:30 pm

Pumpkin Patch Market
10532 US Route 20, two miles west of State Route 5, Middlebury
(574) 825-3312 • pumpkinpatchmarket.com • Monday to Saturday 9 am to 5 pm

Shipshewana Furniture Company
105 East Middlebury Street, Shipshewana • (888) 447-4725
ShipshewanaFurniture.com • Monday to Saturday 9 am to 7 pm

The smallish downtown has shops selling country furnishings, yarn, and goods for cooks; a bakery; and small antique stores. Yoder's Department Store next to the Visitors Center has a dream selection of walking shoes and hiking boots.

✠ pets, etc.

Dogs are allowed but must be on leashes at all times and cannot be taken into restaurants, or restrooms. No alcohol is permitted on the property.

✠ getting there

Shipshewana is 180 miles from Indianapolis, 130 miles from Chicago, and 180 miles from Detroit. Take Exit 107 or 121 from Interstate 80/90 or slow down and drive the back roads.

A note about Indiana's mysterious system of numbering county roads (example: 400 S) may be useful. In each county, small roads are laid out on a grid with the courthouse at the center. Miles are multiplied by 100, so 100 N is 1 mile north of the courthouse and 100 S is 1 mile south. Likewise, 100 E is 1 mile

east, and 100 W is 1 mile west. The intersection of 200 N and 300 W would be 2 miles north and 3 miles west of the courthouse.

Addresses are based on the same system. Here's the test. If Lambright Woodworking is at 7785 W 300 S, where is it? Answer: it is .785 miles west of 700 W on 300 S. Nothing to it. The confusing part is that N and S roads actually travel east/west, while E and W roads travel north/south on the grid, so don't use the system to decide which direction you're going.

ꝏ where to park
Plenty of free parking is available in the front and rear of the market, at nearby businesses, and on side streets. An RV park with 70 hookups is located at Gate 5 on the south side of the market complex. It is open from April to November.

⚓ where to stay

There are many hotels, B&Bs, cabins, and campgrounds nearby. See backroads.org. Rooms book up fast for market days; advance reservations are advised. The closest lodging is the Farmstead Inn and Conference Center directly across the road, 370 S. Van Buren Street, (260) 768-4595, farmsteadinn.com.

⚓ where to eat

Amish are famous for their hearty cooking and baking that is tied to Pennsylvania -Dutch roots. At Amish-run restaurants, stews, roasts, and gravy are served with lots of fresh vegetables. One whoopie pie (thick cream between rounds of choc-olate cake) might be enough for a lifetime. Amish rules apply; alcoholic bev-erages are not available in any restaurants in town, and restaurants are closed on Sunday. Local restaurants serve family-style meals and expect their guests to have good appetites.

Snacks on the market grounds include homemade cotton candy, kettle corn, fudge, and nuts. For a good sit-down lunch four outdoor pavilions serve Amish country food, sandwiches (love the sloppy joes), chicken dinners, and home-made pies. Restrooms and ATM machines are also located here. If you're in the mood for a second dessert, a fellow near the market entrance churns ice cream to order in wooden freezers noisily cranked by a 1919 gasoline engine.

Ben's Bakery

250 E. Berkshire Drive, Shipshewana • (260) 768-4174
Monday to Friday 8 am to 5 pm; Saturday 8 am to 4 pm
Some say these are the best baked goods they've ever eaten; all love the blueberry fry pies.

Blue Gate Restaurant & Bakery

195 N. Van Buren Street, Shipshewana • (260) 768-4725

Monday to Saturday 7 am to 9 pm

Amish cooking and more than 25 kinds of pie; most popular place to eat in town. Restaurants in Shipshewana don't serve alcoholic beverages, so having a drink with dinner means driving to a neighboring town.

Kelly Jae's Café

133 South Main Street, Goshen • (574) 537-1027 • kellyjaescafe.com

Lunch: Wednesday to Friday 11:30 am to 1 pm; Dinner: Tuesday to Thursday 5:30 pm to around 8 pm; Friday and Saturday 5:30 pm to around 8:30 pm; closed Sunday and Monday

Chef/owner Kelly Jae Graff is considered one of Indiana's top chefs. Her specialty is tapas-style dining with an Asian flair. There's a full bar.

Adams Lake Pub

5365 East County Road 620 S, Wolcottville • (260) 854-3463 • adamslakepub.com

Wednesday to Saturday 5 pm to 10 pm; Sunday 8 am to 3 pm; extended bar service available; closed Monday and Tuesday

Locals love the steaks, ribs, and seafood.

Coody Brown's Bar & Grill

1510 East County Road 700 S on Dallas Lake, Wolcottville • (260) 854-2425

Sunday to Friday noon to 8 pm; Friday and Saturday noon to 9 pm; extended bar service available

A lakefront restaurant and night club that serves bar food. Everybody loves the Coody Fries.

✝ nearby attractions

Menno-Hof

510 South Van Buren Street, Shipshewana • (260) 768-4117 • MennoHof.org

September to May: Monday to Saturday 10 am to 5 pm

June to August: Monday to Friday 10 am to 7 pm; Saturday 10 am to 5 pm

Information about the Amish, and their less strict brethren, the Mennonites, can be found at Menno-Hof, a visitor center and museum of the history, faith, and lifestyle of the Amish and Anabaptist. It includes a dungeon, a re-creation of a 17th-century sailing ship, a meetinghouse, and a tornado theater.

Shipshewana/Lagrange County Convention and Visitors Center

350 South Van Buren Street, Suite H • (260) 768-4008 • backroads.org

The Lagrange County Visitors Center provides all the maps and pamphlets a visitor might need. With Amish back roads, little historic towns, and 67 lakes, the county is fun territory to explore.

✝ websites

AmishCountry.org

shipshewana.com

What I bought: a 1950s souvenir pennant from the Ohio Turnpike (where I learned to drive in the fast lane), $5.

What I passed up: two mid-century Bertoia chairs, auction price unknown.

What I will regret forever: a vintage bamboo fly-fishing pole, price unknown.

1350 West Randolph Street and
1340 West Washington Boulevard
(between North Ada Street and
North Ogden Street)
Chicago, Illinois

randolph street market
First weekend in February
Last weekend in March through October
10 am to 5 pm

modern vintage chicago
May and October
See website for dates and times

holiday market
November and December
See website for dates and times

randolphstreetmarket.com

randolph street market festival chicago, illinois

Over in the West Loop near Ogden Park the sassy Randolph Street Market is busy rivaling the Brooklyn Flea. And since we all love great flea markets, that's really good news.

The monthly Randolph Street Market is three events in one—outdoor flea market, Chicago Antique Market, and Indie Designer Market. All happen concurrently in and around Plumbers Hall, an Art Deco union hall where plumbers still meet when the building is not full of antiques or rented out for an event. Vendors come from across the country, some all the way from California.

In warm weather, vendors set up outdoors in the parking lot with antiques, industrial furnishings, kitschy paintings, toys, trinkets, bikes, potted plants, and lots of vintage clothing, hats, and bags. Some of the best outfits seen are those worn by shoppers, head-turning combinations of handmade and vintage clothes with proper eyewear and accessories.

Inside Plumbers Hall, the Chicago Antique Market vendors fill the main level with serious antiques and interesting remade objects involving less serious antiques. The Indie Designer Market takes up the lower level with handmade jewelry, cuddly scarves and shawls, hats, kids' toys and clothes, and home goods. The result is non-stop finds at every price point.

Spring and fall bring Modern Vintage Chicago, a show that has been called the "Barneys of Vintage." It's a fantasy weekend of designer vintage clothing, dazzling estate and vintage jewelry, furs, shoes, and bags. Previews are held on Friday night for the rich and famous and the hoping to be rich and famous.

Holiday Markets in November and December are really parties that include shopping. Find gifts from the mid-19th to the mid-20th centuries, handmade and vintage decorations, and Chicago art. Decorators and stylists offer ideas for fanciful party planning and setting a glam table. Shoppers enjoy Christmas carols, nibbles, chocolate, and cocktails, plus free gift wrapping.

The market charges admission but offers discount tickets online and also season passes, which admit two and include free valet parking for all events. There's also the cheaper Green Pass, admission for two who choose to walk, bike, or take public transportation and don't need valet parking. Students pay less than half price and kids under 12 are free.

⚑ pets, etc.

The market is pet friendly. Dogs must be on leashes and are allowed in the outdoor areas of the market, but not inside Plumbers Hall. Insurance prohibits pit bulls and Dobermans from attending the market.

✠ getting there

A free trolley leaves from the Water Tower Pumping Station, south side of Pearson Street just east of Michigan Avenue, on the hour from 11 am to 3 pm. It departs from the flea on the half-hour. May through September only.

✠ public transportation

Green line train to the Ashland stop. Number 20 bus to Madison and Ashland. The market has two gates, one at 1340 West Washington Boulevard and the other at 1350 West Randolph Street. Out-of-towners might consider leaving the car in a suburban park-and-ride lot and taking the Metro downtown.

✠ where to park

Valet parking is available at the Randolph Street gate, May through September, for a small fee. Free on site parking for events during the rest of the year. Free parking on surrounding streets year round.

✠ where to stay

There are no hotels close to the flea. Rates at hotels in the loop are capricious and vary seasonally. See choosechicago.com. The two hotels below may or may not be affordable but are guaranteed to be special. One is in ultra-trendy Wicker Park; the other is in the Loop close to the free trolley to the flea.

Ruby Room

1743 West Division Street, Wicker Park • (773) 235-2323 • rubyroom.com

This spa/hotel/oasis of pampering and peace boast 600-thread-count sheets and no TVs, spa services, and fringy treatments for the spirit like auratherapy, and a chakra healing. Book well ahead.

The Talbott Hotel

20 East Delaware Place • (800) 825-2688 • talbotthotel.com

Three blocks from the stop for the free trolley to the flea, this circa-1927 building has been updated to green status while preserving the ambiance and décor of the '20s. It's rated among the top ten hotels in Chicago and is a member of Small Luxury Hotels of the World. Book well ahead.

⚑ where to eat

There is a food court at the outdoor market. Beer, wine, and cocktails on the lower level of Plumbers Hall.

Ina's

1235 West Randolph Street • (312) 226-8227 • breakfastqueen.com
Monday to Friday 7 am to 2 pm; Saturday 8 am to 3 pm (breakfast until 2:30 pm); Sunday 8 am to 2 pm (breakfast only)

Ina Pinkney doesn't serve dinner, only breakfast and lunch but mainly breakfast. Her Heavenly Hots (sour cream pancakes with warm fruit) and homemade scrapple are legendary and so is she. Don't miss her many salt and pepper shakers, all gifts from customers. Ina's is one and a half blocks east of the market; free parking.

⚑ nearby attractions

There's not much of interest nearby, but other areas of Chicago are only a few minutes away.

What I bought: a 1941 edition of *Roget's Thesaurus of Words and Phrases*, $5.

What I passed up: a petite Venus flytrap garden, price unknown.

What I will regret forever: a wooden pin of two exotic birds, $75.

Every June on Father's Day weekend
Friday 9 am to 6 pm; Saturday 8 am to 6 pm
Sunday 8 am to 4 pm
walnutantiqueshow.com

walnut antique show
walnut, iowa

Once a year on Father's Day weekend, the AMVETS put on a whale of an antique show in tiny Walnut, Iowa (population 900). Christened Iowa's Antique City, antiques are breakfast, lunch, and dinner here with 20 permanent antique stores and this massive show that draws 20,000 shoppers every year.

AMVETS is a service organization established in 1944 as American Veterans of World War II, with the goal of assisting veterans' return to civilian life. The name was shortened to AMVETS to include servicemen from the Korean War, then Vietnam. The Walnut AMVETS organize and run the antique show from the bottom up, everything from marketing to parking to Porta-potties. During the show Antique City Drive is decorated with American flags, thanks to them.

Walnut started as a water stop on the Chicago, Rock Island, and Pacific Railroad. The first general store opened in 1871. During the next ten years someone started a Sunday school, a doctor came to town, a school and two churches were built, and a newspaper began circulating the local news. By 1880 the population had reached 1,000. The biggest single event in the 20th century was in 1942 when a B-24 bomber crashed south of town. A memorial stands on the spot.

Downtown, the streets are paved with brick and the street lamps are 19th-century-style. Dealers come from 21 states with their very best antiques, and set up along the main thoroughfares, on side streets, and inside town buildings. Expectations are high; such a concentration of quality pieces is rarely seen in the Midwest. There is a rigorous curatorial process. Dealers must submit photos of their merchandise and previous booths. If reviewers are satisfied with the quality, the dealer is monitored for three shows to prove consistency before being allowed to show permanently. The AMVETS are rightly proud of their show, which has been running for more than 30 years.

Some of the sights include ornate Eastlake store fixtures and glass-front display cabinets, original art or needlework in gilded frames, rare clocks, art pottery, seven-foot pier mirrors, photographs of Nebraska homesteaders, obscure kitchen tools for processing farm bounty, early 20th-century toys, davenport desks, chalkware carnival figures, crocks for pickles and jugs for cider, handmade dollhouses, quilts, and antique textiles.

Fragile and small, precious items are in the school building on Antique City Drive near School Street: art glass, fine china, sterling silver, ephemera, lamps, gold and estate jewelry, early fashion illustrations, and antique textiles. Booths are restocked daily with new items.

Although the Antique Show is still the big draw, the junker's movement has hit Walnut. Junk-tober Fest!, a two-day market, debuted in October 2012 with vintage and retro clothing and home goods, and recycled/upcycled antiques.

TrUe JuNk May Daze is the spring show, held on the second weekend in May. See walnutiowa.org for dates and times.

✠ pets, etc.
Pets are allowed.

✠ getting there
Walnut is 87 miles west of Des Moines and 46 miles east of Omaha in the southwest corner of the state, one mile south of I-80 at Exit 46. Antique City Drive (County Road M47) into town can become a nasty traffic jam during the show; alternate routes might be more pleasant. Coming from the west, consider taking Exit 40, Route 59, south to Avoca, then State Highway 83 east to Walnut. From the east take Exit 51 to Marne and turn west on Highway 83 to Walnut.

✠ where to park
Parking is free; follow the signs.

✠ where to stay
A complete list of hotels, B&Bs, and camping facilities is at walnutantiqueshow.com.

✠ where to eat
Community groups make sure everyone at the show gets plenty to eat. The fire department serves breakfast each morning from 6 am to 11 am. The AMVETS Ladies Auxiliary dishes up ham, scalloped potatoes, and pie at the AMVETS Hall all day. Local Girl Scouts give them a hand. The men serve smoked pork loin sandwiches at the AMVETS stand on Atlantic Avenue. Get brats at the

Lutheran Church and Philly steaks at the Rainbow Girls' stand on Main Street south of the school. Friday night there's a sit-down spaghetti supper at the Catholic Church. See a full list of market food stands and local restaurants at walnutantiqueshow.com.

⚓ nearby attractions

Walnut Wind Farm

I-80 in Pottawattamie County, Iowa

Nearing Walnut on I-80, it's impossible to miss the Walnut Wind Farm, 106 towering white wind turbines bordering the highway. The visual impact of these graceful machines comes partly from their contrast against the green farmlands and the blue sky, partly from their size, and partly from their surprising silence. They're beautiful. From ground to tip of blade, each windmill is about 13 stories taller than the top of the Statue of Liberty's torch. Each turbine generates enough electricity annually to power about 350 homes. Lately there's been some discussion around here about whether Walnut is "Antique City" or "Windmill City."

Third weekend in August
Friday and Saturday 7 am to 7 pm;
Sunday 7 am to 2 pm
goldrushmn.com

downtown oronoco gold rush days
oronoco, minnesota

Seventy miles south of Minneapolis there's a flea market that sparkles with great buys, homemade food, and north-country hospitality. For one weekend a year it takes over the entire town of Oronoco, Minnesota, population 1,315. Everybody has a good time and nobody goes home empty-handed.

Oronoco sits among gentle hills beside a quiet river. Legend has it that "in the early days of Oronoco the place was so healthy as to make it necessary to kill a man in order to start a cemetery."

The market has been going on since 1972 when a gentleman named Earl Berg, connecting the tenuous dots between the town's short-lived gold rush in the late 1850s and the rising passion for old stuff, thought something similar to "thar's gold in them thar antiques." And he was right.

The singular aspect of this market is that the whole town volunteers to help run it and all net profits from booth fees and concession stands, sometimes as much as $90,000 a year, go toward supporting the town's infrastructure and residents. The fire department, senior citizen community center, children's park, and churches all benefit. It even pays for the town's Fourth of July fireworks.

There are usually about 350 vendors who spread their wares into every possible corner of town—up and down the three main streets and assorted side streets, through garages and across backyards, around the VFW and the Lutheran church, under trees in the park, and between swing sets in the playground.

The pickings are all-American with a quirky northern flair. From rick-rack-trimmed aprons flying in the breeze to a gaggle of baseball gloves offering high fives, a vintage Gretsch guitar that once belonged to band called Jerry Rigged, to a turquoise Edsel, stacks of Pendleton blankets, and almost enough canoes for 10,000 lakes, it's all there.

pets, etc.
Pets are permitted but it can get crowded so they might not have a good time.

getting there
Minneapolis-St. Paul International (MSP) is the closest airport. Oronoco is 76 miles south, a drive of about one hour and twenty minutes.

where to park
Many Oronoco residents turn their yards into parking lots, and charge a small fee, which is worth it for the convenience. Some people park along the road north of town but it's a hike to the market and no fun when carrying things back to the car.

⚑ where to stay

Rochester, 14 miles south, is the closest city. Accommodations are plentiful because it's home to the Mayo Clinic. See rochesterlodging.com.

⚑ where to eat

The market centers on the firehouse where firefighters and EMT folks serve delicious roast pork sandwiches and never stop pouring the beer. Entertainment comes from an adjoining stage where the likes of the Turkey River All-Stars pick and strut. Over at the VFW the boys make pancakes and sausage under the watchful eye of 92-year-old Commander Don Cooper. Grace Lutheran Church runs the pie booth. Food trucks offer local specialties like cheese curds, fried pickles, and crumble beef sandwiches. Don't even think of leaving without having one of Mama Meg's homemade ice cream sandwiches.

Rainbow Café and Catering

212 South Main Street, Pine Island • (507) 356-2929

Tuesday to Saturday 11am to 8 pm; Sunday 10 am to 1 pm; closed Monday

One exit north. Local grass-fed beef and free-range chicken. Ribeyes, walleye, ribs, salads, burgers, local and craft beer, and an interesting wine list.

Newt's North

5231 East Frontage Road, Upper Level, Rochester • (507) 226-8266 • cccrmg.com

Monday to Thursday 11 am to 11 pm; Friday 11 am to midnight; Saturday 8 am to midnight; Sunday 8 am to 10 pm

Beloved local burger joint with full bar and endless popcorn. Near the hotels at the 55th Street Exit.

Highway 237
from Carmine to La Grange, Texas

spring
Last week of March and
first week of April

fall
Last week of September and
first week of October

antiqueweekend.com

round top/warrenton antiques week
carmine to la grange, texas

Texas. It is entirely possible that for two weeks every year there is no place on earth more fun than Round Top. Five tiny towns are strung together by nobody knows how many antique shows that slip from one marvel to the next for a good 30 miles. Bring your boots, your rhinestones, and your petticoats, and get ready to dance. If you have an Airstream trailer, bring that, too.

The market runs north-south along Highway 237 between Highway 290 and Highway 17 in the lovely Central Texas hill country. It begins near Burton and proceeds through Carmine, Round Top, Shelby, Warrenton, and Fayetteville, ending near La Grange. Shows last for a week to ten days with staggered openings. Shipping and delivery is available along the way. Pick up a copy of *Show Daily* (showdaily.us) for listings, opening and closing dates, maps, and general information.

This all started in 1967 when Miss Emma Lee Turney was asked to put on a little antique show at the Round Top Rifle Association Hall. The show soon became the darling of Houston ladies who belonged to the Garden Club of America and were known as the "mink, martini, and manure" set. Another supporter was Miss Ima Hogg, daughter of Texas governor James Stephen "Big Jim" Hogg, whose commitments to art, preservation, and philanthropy earned her the title "First Lady of Texas." (Her unfortunate first name came from a poem by her uncle. She did not have a sister named Ura.) Now thousands of highly interesting antique and vintage dealers come from all across the country to set up along the route. There are 18 shows in Round Top alone.

Many of the shows revolve around dancehalls, simple clapboard buildings erected by German and Czech immigrants in the late 19th century. Meant for meetings and socializing, they are open to the rafters, crammed with antiques during show weeks, and home to the Texas two-step the rest of the year.

The La Bahia show is first on the north end of the route and a good place to start. It's not too big and is set under a pretty grove of live oaks in the 1879 La Bahia Turn Verein, one of the oldest dance halls in Texas. Inside the stage is deep in flow blue and transferware china, while silver and glassware sparkle under garlands of twinkle lights. Furniture too. There is also quite a bit of shabby including Belle's Best, "Home of the $10 tablecloth."

From there just meander from one show to the next. Some must not be missed. The Original Round Top Antiques Fair is the whopping "show that started it all." The Big Red Barn and Tent are famous for top quality Texas primitives, Americana, and classic antiques including oil paintings, sterling silver, and fine furniture. The Continental Tent is a quick trip to Europe and always has fine pieces. A fourth venue is a few miles away in Carmine at the Carmine

MEN FOR
RENT $ PER HOUR
ONLY AVAILABLE
FOR WOMEN
MOVE FURNITURE

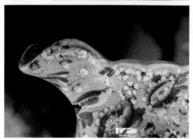

Dance Hall. Look forward to folk art and lots of country furniture. There's a shuttle bus back and forth.

Down the road is Marburger Farm Antique Show, a 43-acre encampment of tents and outbuildings with a wild range of goods arcing all the way from French antiques to American industrial, plus fresh and fearless clothing and jewelry. There are miles of aisles so it helps to pick up a copy of *The Howdy*, a little guide to the show. Admission includes parking on the grounds, and the ticket is good for the duration of the show.

The Ragman is here (he's at Brimfield, too) with his collections of arcane remnants from life in the 19th century. So is Janet Waldrop of Skip 2 My Lou, whose booth in Tent A is impossible to bypass. She makes jewelry out of

things forgotten, then displays it on old photographs with descriptions of the "ingredients" handwritten in gold ink on the back. A will-o'-the-wisp with no website, her show schedule is on her Facebook page.

Also in Tent A, the sartorial style of Magnolia Pearl always creates a stir around the rough and romantic fantasyland they call their booth. Women with cascades of Pre-Raphaelite hair model current designs, which can stretch from the court of Marie Antoinette to Storyville. We saw the Plantation line, white on white over white outfits patched together from bits of antique Victorian undergarments and feed sacks. Expensive but 2 die 4.

Coming into Warrenton, another must stop is at EX-CESS with industrial antiques and its next-door neighbor, Clutter, divine gleanings from England,

Mexico, and the US handpicked by a mother-daughter team. Find them by the red British phone booth in front.

Everybody loves the Zapp Hall Show in the dead center of Warrenton. Known for its funky-flirty pickings, it's anchored by the Junk Gypsies whose accomplishments include styling the wedding of Blake Shelton and Miranda Lambert. Their crowning invention is the Junk-o-Rama Prom, an after-dark event marked by seriously gaudy prom dresses, paste jewels, and boots of all colors.
See junkgypsyblog.com for upcoming dates and times.

⚕ pets, etc.
Show rules vary but it seems that most allow dogs on leashes.

⚴ getting there

The show is midway between Austin and Houston. The closest airport is Austin-Bergstrom, about 71 miles west and on the side of town nearest Round Top. Both airports in Houston are about 85 miles away.

⚴ where to park

Isolated markets have free parking. The major markets charge an admission fee that includes parking and is good for the run of the show. In the crowded areas like Warrenton there are off-street parking areas that charge a fee.

⚴ where to stay

Some say there are no places to stay; others maintain reservations years in advance. In any case, finding a bed is a good trick. The Round Top Chamber of Commerce website, roundtop.org, is a good place to start looking. The Round Antiques Fair site, roundtoptexasantiques.com, also has a useful list. Lodgings range from chain hotels to B&Bs, and cabins to cottages.

Bastrop, 44 miles west of Round Top, has a resort, B&Bs, chain hotels, and a state park with cabins and campgrounds. The distance makes it less desirable to Round Top attendees, so lodgings here are easier to book at the last moment —and it's really only 30 minutes away. See visitbastrop.org.

Brenham, 18 miles east of Round Top, offers a mix of chain hotels and B&Bs. See tripadvisor.com for hotels in Brenham, Texas.

Fayetteville and LaGrange, both just south of Round Top, have many B&Bs and small inns. See the Chamber of Commerce website, fayettevilletxchamber.org.

Round Top has lots of B&Bs, but the ideal location makes them almost impossible to book. See roundtop.org.

⚑ where to eat

Barbeque rules in this part of Texas; some say it's the best in the world. Other local specialties are chicken fried steak and just plain steak. Many shows have food trucks on site; some have satellite locations of local restaurants. Consumption of alcoholic beverages is encouraged and might even be required. A beer, glass of wine, or margarita is available just about anywhere. Shows offer wine and cheese receptions on opening days. Zapp Hall hosts Bargains and Bellinis, an evening of discount shopping with free cocktails. See *Show Daily* for date and time.

Cedar Creek Barbeque at the Carmine Dance Hall Show
Just off Highway 290 in Carmine

Cedar Creek serves traditional German barbeque made with fresh meats and local sausages during the big show in Carmine.

JW's Steakhouse
122 S. Hauptstrasse Street, Carmine • (979) 278-4240 • jw-steakhouse.com
Monday to Thursday 11 am to 9pm; Friday and Saturday 11 am to 10 pm; closed Sunday

If you want a sit-down meal, try the steaks, catfish, and burgers served here.

Royers Round Top Café
105 Main Street, Round Top • (979) 249-3611 • royersroundtopcafe.com
March through August: Wednesday 11 am to 2 pm; Thursday to Saturday

11 am to 9 pm; Sunday noon to 3 pm (see below)

Legendary in this part of Texas, this café's pork tenderloin, rack of lamb, and gulf snapper all have the coveted OMG! rating. The Awesome Steak has a double OMGOMG!! There are a total of ten tables and a wine list with 50 selections. See the website for special antique show hours and reservation details.

Across the street from the Café, Royers Pie Haven is a coffee bar with homemade pies both sweet and savory, breakfast treats, and ice cream.

American Samaritan
Barbeque wagon at the back of Granny McKormick's Yard in Warrenton
Open during show hours

Famous for terrific smoked brisket. Proceeds from sales at the show go to help victims of disasters. Buddy Shipp, who died in 2011, founded American Samaritan in 1991. The idea was simple—take Texas barbeque across the country and feed victims of disasters, first responders, and anyone else who was hungry at no charge. Shipp spent the last year of his life helping earthquake victims in Haiti. "There's nothing you can't do with brisket in your hands," he liked to say.

Royers Round Top Café at Zapp Hall
Inside the Zapp Hall Show in Warrenton • royersroundtopcafe.com
Open during show hours

With a menu that includes shrimp BLT, grilled quail, and the Cutie Pie ("personal sized but world-famous"), this Royers satellite is irresistible not to mention convenient. Lunch and dinner are served every day. Buy a big iced tea and get free refills for the entire length of the show. It's next to Zapp Hall's beer garden and across from the Bubble Lounge, which serves champagne

and has deep couches for dog-tired shoppers. There's live music every night.

Sack Lunch at Clutter

At the rear of Clutter in Warrenton (see page 194), artist and caterer Sharon Bright serves casual, fresh food that isn't "fried or on a stick" from a 1954 Airstream Trailer.

✠ books

Denim and Diamonds: The Story of Emma Lee Turney's Round Top Antiques Fair, by Miss Emma Lee Turney and Beverly Harris.

The Parisian Cowboy's Guide to the Round Top Experience, Parisian Cowboy Publishing.

What I bought: Kitty Dime Savers for all my friends, $5 each.

What I passed up: a baptismal font in working order, price unknown.

What I will regret forever: missing the Junk-o-Rama Prom.

1001 Rose Bowl Drive
Pasadena, California
Second Sunday of every month
Early admission 5 am to 9 am
regular hours 9 am to 3 pm
rgcshows.com

the rose bowl flea market pasadena, california

Remember when being Queen of the Tournament of Roses was only two points lower on the dream scale than being Miss America? And the whole family looked forward to the Rose Parade and the Rose Bowl game? New Year's Day was roses in Pasadena just like Thanksgiving was balloons in New York. It's still the place to be, not just for football fans, but for millions of flea market lovers for whom shopping the Rose Bowl is the bee's knees.

The Rose Bowl is a big white birthday cake of a building decorated with a neon rosette. It sits grandly at the foot of the San Gabriel Mountains. The "Olde Tyme Flea Market" that has been there forever is still sometimes described as a "swap meet." No one seems bothered by the lingo. There's a spot for anyone who wants to sell, whether fine antiques, secondhand ball gowns, chop-o-matics, hand-crocheted baby bonnets, or detritus from the garage.

According to blogs, tweets, and new media, neither mountains nor oceans are obstacles to vendors or shoppers. Girls from Santa Barbara love a certain seller

from Utah; someone stops on her way home to Arizona and fills her car; New Yorkers bring back a small bottle labeled Waldorf Astoria Dry Gin. The same source mentions seeing "every Louis imaginable—from XIII to Vuitton."

The market is laid out with antiques and vintage outside the stadium to the left of the entrance, in the area bounded by Seco Street and West Drive. Antiques and collectibles are in the near sections; vintage is across the canal (look for the bridges). Only new items and arts and crafts are inside the stadium.

Dealers employ all styles of display, whether elegantly arranged antiques in faux room settings, wooden boxes filled with tiny trinkets, cowboy boots lined up on sagging boards, or the dump-truck aesthetic where everything is flung out of the car onto a blanket on the ground. Demand for dealer space in the antiques area is so high that spaces coming vacant are auctioned to the highest bidder.

The flea is a haunt for film, fashion, and costume designers who come early and sweep up some of the best pickings. Major celebrities like to shop too and are spotted all the time. A short list includes Heidi Klum, Diane Keaton, Gwen Stefani, Clint Eastwood, Paula Abdul, Jessica Alba, Whoopi Goldberg, Emily Henderson, Jeremy Scott, Kat Von D, Barbra Streisand, Nicole Richie, Maria Shriver, Jason Priestley, Rod Stewart, and Cher.

A word to describe the number of vintage dresses here has not yet been coined. Racks and racks stretch from booth to booth until they whirl off in a kaleidoscopic vision of ironic prints and polka dots. A little game might be to buy one item of vintage clothing, then try to find everything else needed to make a complete outfit. This could be amusing as a short-lived reality show, or take several visits to the market to accomplish.

Whatever one might collect, or dare we say hoard, is probably here in multiples. Old technology may not be first on everyone's list, but those who search for film cameras, ham radios, or tube testers may find exactly what they want. Sports memorabilia is another category not so easily found at other shows. How about a restored Vespa? There would be no problem getting it home.

And what about the real antiques? Courtly and solid, they know what they are and cannot be intimidated by upstarts of the 1930s or party girls of the 1970s. Humph, say they, and wait for just the right buyer.

It would take days to see everything, and with the box office closing at 3 pm there is a time limit here. If you prefer an organized approach, have someone show you around the market. Peek offers the Finders Reapers tour, an insider-bypass-the-lines-and-meet-the-vendors guided tour. See peek.com or call (855) PEEK-TRAVEL. For general information see visitpasadena.com.

⚓ pets, etc.
Pets are not allowed.

⚓ getting there
Take the 110 Freeway from downtown Los Angeles, the 134 Freeway if coming from the west, and the 210 Freeway if coming from the east or northwest. See rosebowlstadium.com for detailed directions. Bob Hope Airport in Burbank (BUR) is the closest and purports to be hassle-free.

⚓ where to park
There is free parking on the Rose Bowl grounds, plus preferred parking near the entrance for a fee. Follow the signs.

⚓ where to stay

Langham Huntington Hotel

1401 South Oak Knoll Avenue, Pasadena • (626) 568-3900

pasadena.langhamhotels.com

This dreamy period hotel sits on 23 acres of landscaped grounds near the San Gabriel Mountains, and is close to the Rose Bowl. It's not as expensive as it looks.

The Saga Motor Hotel

1633 East Colorado Boulevard, Pasadena • (626) 795-0431, (800) 793-7242

thesagamotorhotel.com

This inexpensive vintage hotel with a history and a beautiful pool is located on Colorado Avenue, the Rose Parade route and formerly Route 66. Built in 1957, remodeled in 2011, the Saga is loved by some, not by others, but is easy on the budget regardless.

⚓ where to eat

Julia Child was born in Pasadena and the current culinary crowd takes this very seriously. See visitpasadena.com for suggestions on the best places to eat and drink.

Food is plentiful at the market and falls into the typical state fair/football stadium category including breakfast pastries, burgers, hot dogs, fries, barbeque, pizza, and burritos. Lighter fare includes rice bowls and sushi. Cocktails, beer, and wine are available.

2900 Navy Way at Main Street
Alameda, California
First Sunday of every month
6 am to 3 pm

auction

Michaan's Auction Gallery
2751 Todd Street
Alameda, California
First Sunday of the month
10 am

alamedapointantiquesfaire.com

alameda point antiques faire
alameda, california

For sale—one million cool objects on an island overlooking San Francisco Bay.

With history's razzmatazz spread out over a thousand acres right across the Bay from San Francisco, Alameda Point offers the difficult choice of getting lost among the hundreds of vendors, or just sitting by the water and relishing the view. Or both.

The Faire is at the former Alameda Naval Air Station, a vast abandoned World War II airfield on the western tip of Alameda Island that has often been used as a location for filming car chases and staging explosions. The site is completely flat and the market seemingly endless; one could browse for hours and not see half of it.

Alameda Point has had its moments in history. In 1935 25,000 people stood on this spot and cheered as the most romantic airplane ever, the Pan Am China Clipper, took off on its maiden voyage to Manila. Narrowly missing the Bay Bridge, it cleared the Golden Gate and, after seven days and four stops, became

the first commercial airplane to cross the Pacific Ocean. In about five minutes America was flooded with Clipper memorabilia; some might even turn up here at the Faire.

Dealers and goods are multinational, coming from the Americas, Europe, and Asia. All items must be at least 20 years old; some things date before 1900, but much of the merchandise comes from the first 80 years of the 20th century. Early furniture styles—Arts and Crafts, Art Nouveau, and art deco are well represented. Mid-Century Modern is probably the hottest style but some people do come for the French Country.

Vintage pickings are inexhaustible. In every category from textiles and linens to clothing, bags, hats, and shoes, from toys and games to kitchen and bath hardware and utensils, and vinyl records, there's a wonderland of possessions, high and low design, and beautiful irrelevant technology.

Although the site is huge, organizers make it easy to navigate and shop. Each row of booths is clearly marked by a letter of the alphabet. Shopping carts are available for a small rental fee. A section is set aside for pick-up near the main entrance with flat bed carts for hauling, a loading zone for cars and trucks, and friendly staff to help with lifting.

There are two schools of thought on arrival time, early to get the best pickings and park close to the entrance, or later to avoid traffic and get the best deals. The Faire offers early entrance from 6:00 am to 7:30 pm at a higher admission price for those who like to browse at daybreak. The website has directions to less congested routes for ten o'clock scholars. One veteran shopper advises that no matter what time you get there, you will get a good deal.

The Michaan family, the show's organizer, has an auction gallery just down the street where major art, antique, and jewelry auctions are held during the Faire. There's shuttle service between the Faire and the auction so you only have to park once. Previews are typically held on the Friday and Saturday before the Faire. See michaans.com for upcoming auctions.

ꓭ pets, etc.
Neither pets nor smoking are permitted.

ꓭ getting there
The market is close to Oakland International Airport, and easily reached from Oakland via the Webster Street Tube or any of four bridges. Public transportation from the city includes BART (the train) plus bus, or the San Francisco Bay Ferry. Complete directions, maps, and alternate routes are posted on the Faire's website.

ꓭ where to park
Parking is free in a lot so big there's complimentary shuttle service to the market entrance.

ꓭ where to stay
Several nearby hotels offer discount rates to Faire goers.
See alamedapointantiquesfaire.com under Alameda Info.

ꓭ where to eat
San Francisco has some of the most outrageous food trucks in the country, for both culinary and decorative reasons. On market Sundays they line up alongside the booths and get cooking. For starters imagine venison sliders, truffle fries, mini-pies

in a jar, kale Caesar salad, fried oyster mushrooms, steamed bao with pork belly and pickled daikon, alligator jerky, orange miso chicken wings, and Nutella crepes.

⚓ where to drink

Forbidden Island Tiki Lounge

1304 Lincoln Avenue, Alameda • (510) 749-0332 • forbiddenislandalameda.com
Monday to Thursday 5 pm to midnight; Friday and Saturday 5 pm to 2 am;
Sunday 3 pm to 10 pm

It might be hard to skip this sanctuary of 1960s island décor co-owned by a former bartender at Trader Vic's. On Sundays it opens at 3 pm, just as the flea market is closing.

What I bought: antique Chinese school children's bench, $200.

What I passed up: antique porch swing, $300.

What I will regret forever: pair of authentic French leather club chairs, $1,200.

spring fling junk fest
Embassy Suites Portland-Airport
7900 North East 82nd Avenue,
Portland, Oregon
One weekend in late March or early April

summer junk fest
McMenamins Edgefield
2126 South West Halsey Street,
Troutdale, Oregon
One day in mid-August

holiday junk fest
Embassy Suites Portland-Airport
7900 North East 82nd Avenue,
Portland, Oregon
One weekend in mid-to-late November

pluckymaidens.com or
facebook.com/PluckyMaidens

plucky maidens junk fest portland, oregon

The Plucky Maidens consider four things essential to a first-rate flea market—junk, food, cocktails, and music. And pluck of course. "I believe the word plucky has been missing from the English lexicon far too long," says show organizer Pam Knecht, who is joined by scores of vendors from the immediate area and beyond. Reviewing their wares, it's apparent there's very little they haven't thought of, scrounged, made, decorated, or baked. Plucky is as plucky does.

Knecht started Plucky Maidens in 2011 in order to bring vintage to Portland. It belongs to the new generation of flea markets where old things are valued more for their ravished beauty than their monetary worth, and it's generally believed by both vendor and shopper that a coat of paint, a metallic marker, and a tube of Rub 'n' Buff can improve just about anything. Add wit, humor, and a pair of jeweler's pliers to the junker's tool kit and the humblest objects can attain star status. We don't call this style Shabby Chic anymore; we call it Neo-Plucky.

The Spring Fling Junk Fest pops up with the tulips toward the end of March or early in April. The date is announced as soon as arrangements are finalized. Early spring markets always have the best things since the vendors have been collecting and crafting for months. Just seeing this colorful vintage spread after the long gray winter is restorative. Expect lots of clothes, shoes, dishes, and things to sparkle up the kitchen and bath, all arranged in perfect vignettes.

What junker can resist creepy old county homes and abandoned asylums? Edgefield, Portland's former poor farm, was a shambling complex with lots of ungainly outbuildings. It sat empty for years until the brothers McMenamin, who occupy a niche market of making the weird weirder, managed to bring it back with an eye that united hospitality, art, and history. Now it's McMenamins Edgefield, a resort hotel with 100 rooms, pubs, spa, movie theater, gardens, golf courses, brewery, and many well-documented ghosts. The buildings and grounds are embellished with murals and sculptures by artists-in-residence who call their style "historical surrealism." Just the place for the Maidens' summer junk fest, which takes place there every August.

This time the market is outdoors. It's a real kick-out-the-jams party with cocktails, live music, and lots and lots of junk. With martinis in hand, shoppers breath deeply, say a quick thank you to the Goddess of Glitter, and dive right in. Besides the regular stuff like furniture—original or refabbed, industrial metal whats-its, French canisters, cowgirl novels, hankies, gloves 'n' buttons, typewriters, fussy aprons, etc., etc., etc., someone has planted tiny succulent gardens in rusty flour sifters. The girls of Camp Hollyhock are showing their pretty clothes made entirely of old linens and frayed tablecloths. Sugar Shapes is selling fresh-baked cookies that look like Ball canning jars. It seems that

imagination has r-u-n-n-o-f-t with American junk.

In November the Holiday Junk Fest is at the Embassy Suites near the Portland Airport. Plucky shoppers can fly in, do all their holiday shopping, and fly right back out, or take a nice break and stay for Thanksgiving. The finds here range from junk, enhanced junk, spectacular gifts, and precious household treasures to mid-century aluminum Christmas trees with or without rainbow wheels, bushels of ornaments, and many incarnations of Santa. There might even be boxes of that old lead tinsel that hangs so nicely on the tree.

Continuing their high jinks the Plucky Maidens like to shop the fleas in Europe. Each year Knecht organizes spring junk jaunts to Paris. In the fall it's London. She adores travel, has lived in Paris, speaks French, and says she's "tickled glittery pink" to lead the trips each year. A New York trip has been added to the schedule.

In Paris the group shops the flea markets at Porte de Clingnancourt, Porte de Vanves, Porte de Montreuil, and sometimes local venues, visits the flower market on the Seine, and has other adventures like wandering through the Montparnasse Cemetery and having a "wine-soaked lunch" at the Luxembourg Gardens.

The London tour includes Bermondsey Square Antiques Market, Old Spitalfields Market, and the Jubilee Market at Covent Garden. Knecht says, "Shoppers can also go to Portobello Road if they choose to, but it's not part of the Plucky package. No bargains there, and not enough JUNK!" At least one museum or famous church is included and, of course, a proper English tea.

Pluckiness continues on Knecht's prizewinning blog, One Gal's Trash. onegalstrash.blogspot.com

✠ pets, etc.

Embassy Suites allows pets as overnight guests but they are not allowed in the ballroom so can't go to the market. Edgefield does not allow pets at all.

✠ getting there

Portland International Airport (PDX) is next door to the Embassy Suites Portland Airport and 10 minutes from the summer market at Edgefield.

✠ parking

There is plenty of free parking at both market locations.

✠ where to stay

Since all three markets are at hotels, lodging couldn't be easier.

Embassy Suites Portland-Airport

7900 Northeast 82nd Avenue • (503) 460-3000 • embassysuites.hilton.com

Discount room rates are offered to Plucky people at this hotel.

McMenamins Edgefield

2126 South West Halsey Street • Troutdale, Oregon • (503) 669-8610, (800) 669-8610 • mcmenamins.com

Pick up a map of the property and explore the hotel and gardens. See the pottery studio in what used to be the morgue, have a cocktail in the former fumigation station, and visit the 7-foot arboreal statue of Jerry Garcia.

⚓ where to eat

Since food is one of the Plucky requirements, there is plenty to eat at all the markets. The restaurant and all the pubs at McMenamins are open during the August show.

⚓ nearby attractions

Columbia River Gorge National Scenic Area
crgva.org

Columbia Gorge Discovery Center and Wasco County Museum
5000 Discovery Drive • The Dalles, Oregon • (541) 296-8600
gorgediscovery.org

If junk isn't enough reason to visit Portland, some of the best scenery in America is just to the east where the Columbia River spends 75 gorgeous miles passing through the Cascade Mountains. One side of the gorge is in Oregon, the other in Washington. Scenic highways on both sides pass 21 parks, 89 waterfalls, 54 hiking trails, 50 wineries, and one live volcano (Mt. Hood). Campgrounds, hotels, and restaurants are all along the way. The area is famous for kayaking, fishing, hiking, and skiing.

What I bought: a "Dreaming of Junking" calendar from the Vintage Rescue Squad, $15.

What I passed up: many doll's heads, various prices.

What I will regret forever: purple cowgirl boots, price unknown.

Spokane County Fair and Expo Center
404 North Havana Street
Spokane Valley, Washington
First weekend in June
Saturday 9 am to 6 pm
Sunday 9 am to 4 pm
thefarmchicks.com

the farm chicks antique show
spokane valley, washington

If a market can be considered a masterpiece, Farm Chicks is a contender. Just ask the besotted fans who come from all over the world to attend this show in Spokane. The line forms early, but no one minds waiting. The fun has already begun with the anticipation of being let loose in aisles and aisles of funky finds. "It just makes me giddy happy to be here," laughs one woman.

The unwritten theme is Americana resurrected. It's where you go for a beat-up galvanized bucket that could hold magazines next to a claw-foot bathtub, a broken ladder to make a coat rack for the mud room, a wheelbarrow with flat tires to use as an ice bucket at family picnics, rusty bedsprings for lamp bases, feed sacks for curtains, maybe even a broken-down VW van for an outdoor (or indoor if the house is big enough) mini-office. If imagination fails, the resourceful vendors are there to assist.

At this point the show has spots for 300 vendors. Each one has passed a curatorial review and is a bona fide Farm Chick. All have sharp eyes for antiques and are quick to see the bright light of usefulness hidden under the shadow of neglect. Many do only this show and spend the entire year collecting for it. And all must agree to be friendly; there are no crabby vendors here.

Don't go for traditional antiques or sleek mid-century modern furniture. Ideal dreamwares are hard-luck leavings from vanishing places: general stores, feed stores, dime stores, textile mills, one-room schoolhouses, tourist courts, trolley cars, lake cottages, red barns, front porches, and old farm kitchens with linoleum floors and cast-iron stoves. Most items date from the 1930s through the 1960s.

Besides vernacular architectural details and furniture, there is plenteous antique and vintage adornment for both home and body in the categories of linens, curtains, signs, paintings, prints, dishes, glassware, toys, frocks, jewelry, and accessories. A few vendors even mix in a bit of French country.

The woman behind this is tastemaker Serena Thompson, who has become a celebrity in the world of creative country living. It actually was *Country Living*, the magazine, which provided the needed leap into the mainstream by discovering the show, writing a feature article, and inviting her to become a contributing editor. She lives in the country outside Spokane.

Serena started junking earlier and more devoutly than most. Her parents were hippies and the family lived in a gypsy wagon, then a cabin without electricity or plumbing. Whatever they needed, they found by prowling dumps and junk heaps. She learned to sew and cook and play with what they scavenged and never forgot the lessons learned.

Later, as a married lady with kids, she recruited friend Teri Edwards and together they searched creaky farm buildings, rescuing the best of the broken

and rusty. Next came a rummage sale in a friend's barn that drew unexpected attention, and prompted a graduation to grange halls. As the crowds grew to thousands, the show settled into the county fairgrounds and began to attract national attention.

Looking at Serena's blog, thefarmchicks.typepad.com, the Chicks' Facebook page, and all the related blogs and posts gives an idea of how much fun everyone has at this show. On her website, myfavoritefind.com, junkers share their most memorable purchases.

For those who can't wait for the next show The Farm Chicks have an online shop at their website that sells cooking and baking supplies, books on cooking and decorating, and their own two books, *The Farm Chicks in the Kitchen: Live Well, Laugh Often, Cook Much* by Serena Thompson and Teri Edwards, and *The Farm Chicks Christmas: Merry Ideas for the Holidays* by Serena Thompson.

⚲ pets, etc.

Pets are not allowed at the fairgrounds.

⚲ getting there

The show is held indoors at the Spokane County Fair and Expo Center, 17 minutes east of Spokane International Airport (GEG). Admission is charged; advance tickets can be purchased the day before the show at the fairgrounds, or anytime during the show.

⚲ where to park

Parking at the fairgrounds is easy and free.

⚲ where to stay

There's a list of recommended hotels at thefarmchicks.com. Serena's favorite is the historic Davenport Hotel in downtown Spokane. The fairgrounds' management offers discounted rates at partner hotels; see spokanecounty.org. Camper and RV parking with water and electricity hook-ups is also available on-site. It's no surprise that the newish sport of glamping (glamorous camping) is very much in evidence here.

Davenport Hotel
10 South Post Street • (800) 899-1482 • davenporthotelcollection.com

⚲ where to eat

Eats at the show are catered by the fairground management and consist of the usual fair foods. The exception is homemade baked goods from a local chef who is part of a seven-sister baking family and brings goodies to every show. See thefarmchicks.com for Serena's suggestions for dining after the show.

Skyway Café
6105 E. Rutter Avenue • (509) 534-5986 • skywaycafe.com
Monday 6 am to 3 pm; Tuesday to Saturday 6 am to 9 pm; Sunday 7 am to 3 pm

Note to spouses, partners, and significant others: If the show is not your cup of tea, head to nearby Skyway Café for coffee and a memorable breakfast. It's at Felts Field, a 1913 airfield that's on the National Register of Historic Places. The restaurant is decorated with antique aircraft memorabilia, and diners can watch small airplanes and helicopters taking off and landing while enjoying huge pancakes, specialty omelets, and fresh cinnamon rolls.

✈ nearby attractions

Carr's One of a Kind in the World Museum

5225 North Freya, Spokane • (509) 489-8859

Saturday 1 pm to 4 pm; Sunday 1 pm to 3 pm (call to verify)

Most junkers will completely understand Marvin Carr's personal museum of unique finds. Roadside America rates it "Major Fun." Carr gives personal tours to all visitors so he can properly show off his replica of a 17th-century warship made of matchsticks, Jackie Gleason's car, an opium pipe found in the ruins of the San Francisco earthquake, two stuffed squirrels driving a miniature fire engine, and an electrocuted boa constrictor, all of which might be One of a Kind in the World. He, of course, is One of a Kind too.

NOV 2013

acknowledgements

I would like to thank all the vendors, dealers, organizers, and market managers who let me take pictures, tolerated me poking around, and answered my questions. Some of them are: The Ragman and all my old friends at Brimfield; Eric Demby of the Brooklyn Flea along with Old Croak Antiques, The Gifted Putterer, Keith Lowery of Hunters and Gatherers, David Sokosh of Brooklyn Watches, and Dan Treiber and his parents' house; and Tony Soprano, undaunted organizer of the miraculous Phila Flea, where I was nourished by Sister Waheedah's fine carrot pies.

Patricia McDaniel who founded the Historic National Road Yard Sale sent me on my way to fabulous finds among silos and cornfields and a barn where they were grilling luscious pork chops. In Atlanta, I had fun with Jo Ann Rogers of Grosgrain Annie's Ribbon Emporium, Sabrina Orangio (so then…so now), and Robin Renner Doty at Remains of War whose specialty is historical conflicts, just like me. At Renninger's, General Manager R. Doyle Carlton showed me around and introduced me to camera guy Robert Cauthen, jewelers Francis and Linelle Lynch, and incorrigible collectors David Law and Ed Atzenhoffer. I wish Molly from Raleigh was my fairy godmother.

Jeff Scofield got me started at Round Top, Skip 2 My Lu and Magnolia Pearl got me in the mood, and the bottomless iced tea from Royer's Café at Zapp Hall kept me going. Pam Knecht and her Plucky Maidens and Farm Chick Serena Thompson were inspirational in the Northwest. Bistrot Lepic in Georgetown won my heart with their hospitality and unforgettable *île flottante*, and the

about the author

Pamela Keech has been addicted to flea mark... watched her father buy a 19th-century Stein... writer, and expert in the material cultu... began working as Curator of Furnishi... furnished the entire museum with f... *Shopper's Guide to New York C*... *Guide to Rome*. She lives in New Y... www.pamelakeech.com

Mutiny Hotel in Miami was perfect.

Endless thanks to Angela Hederman, brilliant publisher and old friend, and the Little Bookroom crew of magicians who led me through the maze of airplanes and rental cars, words and photographs, to create an actual book. I would have faded without April, Sheree, Maddy, Meg, Lisa, Arnhild, Helene, Patty Ann, my car Mavis, and especially my dear old Nick who didn't quite make it to the finish.